CACTUS

W9-AQC-237

Elisabeth Manke

CACTUS

The Most Beautiful Species and Their Care

BARRON'S

Contents

A Word in Advance . . .

Cacti, like no other group of plants, are such favorites that one always wants to have more than one. Anyone who has been bitten by the bug stays hooked on cacti. But what is it that fascinates us about these sometimes downright ugly plants? Why can't we give them up? The spiny plants, which differ enormously from other houseplants, have many virtues: First of all, their toughness has made them legendary. In fact, they are probably the only indoor plants that, more often than not, do not die even when neglected and given minimal care. In addition to the fascination of their frequently odd shape and spination, their wonderful flowers charm us with their glowing colors and delicacy in contrast to the stout and sturdy plant bodies. In order to be able to enjoy this captivating splendor and uniqueness, we need some basic information on the proper care of cacti. Of course, we must not "nurse them to death" either. As always, the correct way is to be found somewhere in the middle. This book offers tips and advice on the various genera, especially for beginners. But even the advanced cactus lover will surely find something worth knowing—be it of history or native habitat—about his or her cactus here.

This book is presented as a guide for the care and maintenance of all important and common representatives of the huge family of Cactaceae (cactus plants) as houseplants. At the same time, the book lays no claim to completeness, since new discoveries are still being made and there is much to be said about cacti.

There is such an abundance of these plants that it is hard for any author to present an inventory that includes, to some degree, not only well-known and common varieties but also those as yet unknown and, perhaps for this very reason, interesting. I have tried to do this with the idea that my book will be not only informative but fun to read.

For many different reasons, in the past the naming of cacti had undergone a multitude of revisions and changes, and this continues to be the case to the present day. As a result, it is not easy for cactus lovers to find their way around in the confusion of names. I have, therefore, used the following as the basis for a reassuring nomenclature: Fritz, Encke; Günther, Buchheim; Siegmund, Seybold: Zander, Handwörterbuch der Pflanzennamen [Concise Dictionary of Plant Names], 15th edition, published by Eugen Ulmer, Stuttgart, Germany, 1994. All those names that are no longer current but are on the CITES list are also mentioned.

The whole cactus family is protected under the 1974 Washington Convention on International Trade in Endangered Species of Wild Fauna and Flora (CITES). So that these interesting and, in some cases, very rare plants do not disappear entirely some day, collecting them from the wild, damaging them, and dealing in them are prohibited. The CITES list includes all those species that are seriously threatened with extinction. Every reliable cactus dealer gives the buyer a so-called CITES certificate stating that the cactus does not come from the threatened natural habitat, but from propagation.

Elisabeth Manke, Zarrendorf, 1998

Page 4: Cacti need lots of light and can do without much space.

What Are Cacti?

Cacti belong to the large group of fleshy (succulent) plants. They form a clearly defined group of dicotyledons that, with one exception, the genus *Rhipsalis,* all come from the American continent. Cacti have fleshy thick stems and branches, sometimes even leaves (e.g., *Pereskia*), in a great many variations. They store water in them and use it only very sparingly. Cacti develop a tremendous suction pressure with their rootage. Their well-developed fibrous root system draws moisture from the soil at up to 147.15 bar suction. In comparison with other plants, cacti have a very small surface and only perhaps one-tenth the number of stomata of other plants. As a result, their evaporation is very limited. This is how they can survive long dry periods without difficulty. Although cacti are no longer firm and bright green after such a dry period, but become quite shriveled, they nevertheless suffer no damage and are able to recover. This phenomenon can be observed every year in the winter, when cacti are kept cool (average of 40–45°F [5–8°C]) and relatively dry.

Their fleshiness (succulence) also permits survival of the plants during winter dormancy. This is when cacti set their buds. If they are not kept cool and dry, they do not have many flowers.

In addition, for protection against evaporation cacti have a thick waxy layer and a coat of spines that protects them from the damage of strong sun.

Cacti are flowering plants that can differ greatly in appearance. Some have the shape of a ball and remain tiny, with a diameter of $\frac{1}{2}$ to $1\frac{1}{2}$ inches (1 to 2 cm). But there are also cactus balls that weigh several tons. Others form columns up to 65 feet (20 m) high (e.g., *Carnegiea*) or look like heavily branched trees with huge crowns (for instance, among *Myrtillocactus*). Still others have snakelike stems, such as *Selenicereus.*

Many cacti grow to form broad cushions or impenetrable thickets. Most of them are equipped with sharp and often very attractive spines (not thorns). In some, one cannot even tell that they have spines, because these have been converted to other parts on the stem or can be found only as hairlike bristles. Others have a woolly, soft covering of hair.

INFO

Cacti are protected under the Washington Convention on International Trade in Endangered Species of Wild Fauna and Flora (Appendix II) of 1974. So, no digging them up while on vacation! Species that are threatened with extinction are also listed (Appendix I) in this Convention.

Left: *Echinopsis mamillosa* var. *kermesina* has surprisingly large flowers (7 inches [18 cm]). It was discovered in Bolivia in 1938.

Page 6: The fine white bundles of spines of *Opuntia microdasys* are just as striking as its delicate yellow flowers.

Where Do Cacti Come From?

The area of distribution of cacti ranges from 56° latitude north to 52° latitude south of the American continent (only *Rhipsalis* is also at home in Africa). This huge area covers some 4,600,000 square miles (2 million km²). It ranges from the Rocky Mountains in Canada through the whole American continent all the way to Patagonia near the Strait of Magellan. Cacti grow primarily in plains, semideserts, and deserts, but also in tropical rain forests—particularly epiphytic genera. Relatively few are found in moist coastal regions, *Melocactus* being one example.

Some cacti live on flatlands, but others—and this applies to most of them—are pronounced mountain dwellers; they can be found in the Andes of Peru, Bolivia, and Chile at heights of up to 15,700 feet (4,800 m) above sea level. The highlands of Mexico are an additional main area of distribution of cacti.

Left: *Carnegiea gigantea,* which can be found in the United States (California, Arizona) at up to 4,800 feet (1,219 m) above sea level and in the Mexican state of Sonoma, is branched like a candelabra.

Page 8: Such huge masses as here in northern Mexico are seldom attained by *Ferocactus pilosus* in the home or greenhouse.

Bottom left: *Echinocereus triglochidiatus* produces edible red fruits. This plant is widely distributed in the south of the United States and in Mexico.

Bottom right: *Opuntia basilaris* can be found in the southwestern United States as well as in Mexico.

How Do Cacti Grow?

Growth Habits

Cacti are divided into three subfamilies, according to growth habit. The leaves are modified to various degrees and usually are present only in the form of spines. The latter are found at the axillary buds, the **areoles,** from which branches or flowers are produced. The most primitive cacti are the **Pereskioideae,** with true flat or fleshy leaves, which usually only last for one growing season. They generally grow as climbers in open, dry woodlands. Some resemble medium-sized deciduous trees, for example, *Pereskia.*

Although **Opuntioideae** still put out true leaves on the primary stem, they soon lose these. Their often heavily spined areoles almost always bear fine barbed hairs (glochids). The flowers are saucer-shaped, never funnel-shaped or tubular.

The **Cactoideae** are the subfamily of cacti with the largest number of species. They no longer bear leaves on the main stem, and their body shapes vary greatly. They have ribs that are more or less characteristic of the habit and in many cases are modified into tubercles or warts typical of a genus. In some genera the growing points, the **axils,** from which the flowers arise, lie at the base. They are often surrounded by axillary wool or a **cephalium** (see photograph on page 153). Cacti come in a great variety of shapes, and there are some interesting curiosities, such as the crested or cristate form (*forma cristata*). There the punctiform vegetative cone at the apex of the cactus is modified to form a band, so that

Page 10: This beautiful cactus collection gives a good general picture of the many different growth habits of cactus.

Left: The prickly pear has flat rounded stems ("pads"): *Opuntia microdasys,* coming from Mexico, has bunches of glochids instead of spines.

Bottom: Bishop's Caps (*Astrophytum*) are at home in southern Texas and Mexico.

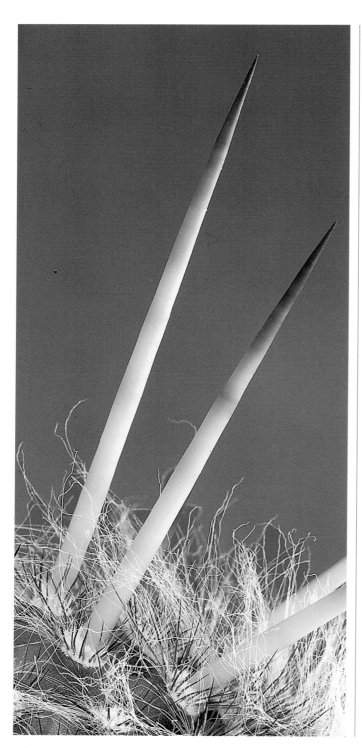

multiple winding ridges often are produced by this banding (see photograph on page 153, bottom). As yet nothing certain is known about the cause of this interesting phenomenon, which occurs in cacti through-out all genera.

Spination

The most striking features of cacti, however, are their **spines,** which also give these plants their unique appearance. The spines in cacti are modified leaves. In addition to spines, scales, bristles, or hairs also develop from such leaf systems. Hence none of these are structures of the outer skin (epidermis), as thorns are in the case of roses, for instance. Spines vary greatly in shape. Apart from their various sizes—from small spines, barely visible to the naked eye, up to spikes 1 foot (30 cm) long—their shape is also very variable: needlelike, awl-shaped, hairlike, conical, spearlike, papery, ridged, hooked, feathery, straight, flat, or round. Cactus spines may also be found as long hairs, as bristles, or as down.

In addition, there are genera that basically have no spines, like *Rhipsalis, Epiphyllum, Lophophora,* and others. Others, on the contrary, have a very thick spinal integument, such as *Echinocactus* and *Mammillaria,* for example. The color of the spines also varies from species to species, and it likewise varies with increasing maturity. It ranges from black through brown, red, and yellow all the way to white and is an integral element in the beauty of many kinds of cactus.

In addition to being a defense against voracious enemies, spines also have a very practical significance: In particular, the finer ones collect moisture—for example, evening dew—and absorb it. Since the surface of the spines as a whole is relatively great in some varieties of cactus, the quantity of liquid collected is vitally important.

Top left:
Some species of
Mammillaria have
hooked, projecting
central spines.

Top right:
*Echinocactus gru-
sonii* has extremely
hard, easily bent radi-
al and central spines
that intersect one an-
other.

Center left:
Pelecyphora displays
pectiniform spines re-
sembling woodlice.

Bottom left: The cen-
tral spine is often
larger and projects
from the radial spines
in, for example,
Melocactus.

Left: The spines in
*Mammillaria
spinosissima* are
fine bristles.

Page 12: How differ-
ent in shape the
spines may be can be
clearly seen in this
Espostoa: a stout,
very large central
spine and many short,
fine bristles at the
margin of the areoles,
as well as delicate
hairlike spines.

Native Habitat

The kinds of soil in which cacti thrive are just as variable: They range from the moist humus of the tropical rain forest through the clay soil of plains and woodlands all the way to the sand and scree of deserts. Cacti even live in pure quartz sand such as in northeastern Brazil and in Campo Rupestre, where the genera *Melocactus, Uebelmannia,* and *Pilosocereus* are found. Most cacti, however, make their homes in the south of the United States, in Mexico, Brazil, Bolivia, Chile, and Argentina, where there are extensive desert areas and semideserts full of cactus. Temperatures in these areas range from more than 125°F (51.7°C) all the way to regions near the frost line. Cacti are able to withstand such extremes without any problem, because it is dry during the cold period. The cell sap of the plants becomes concentrated

(shrinks) and the freezing point is reduced. The plant body is so shriveled that the watery cell sap, should it freeze, still has enough room to expand without harming the plant.

Flowers
The cactus family generally has very odd shapes, but its flowers are often exceptionally beautiful. They are produced singly or multiply in a particular region of the plant, the cephalium, which is striking for its dense formation of hairs, bristles, or even wool. The only flower color absent in cactus is pure blue. White, pink, red, and yellow are found in many variants. There are day-flowering cacti that are intense in color, in order to attract insects and birds (especially hummingbirds) for pollination. Night-flowering cacti develop a strong fragrance, with which they attract moths and other insects and even bats for pollination.

History of Discovery
Cacti reached Europe through the discovery of America. The botanist Carolus Linnaeus (1707–1778) placed all the cacti that he had in one genus, *Cactus.* At that time, only 20 species were known to him. Today we are familiar with more than 1,600 species in some 130 genera.

Page 14 top: Flat, wide open flower of *Opuntia hystricina.*

Page 14 bottom left: The beautiful, large, cream-colored flower of this *Epiphyllum* hybrid opens at night.

Top left: With its decorative stamens, this *Epiphyllum* hybrid blooms just as beautifully but in a different color.

Bottom left: This *Matucana aureiflora* has zygomorphous (bilaterally symmetrical) flowers.

Bottom: A *Schlumbergera* hybrid is an example of a cactus flower with a long flower neck.

Cacti in the Home

Whether because they are easy to care for or because they surprise us again and again with their lovely flowers, cacti have always enjoyed great popularity as house-plants. Or are cacti so popular because they do not need much space? A win-dowsill will accommodate a fair number of these plants. Besides, cacti, more than any other plants, teach us to be patient. It takes seemingly forever until one notices any changes (i.e., indications of growth) at all, in most species. But as extravagant as cacti are with time, so are they thrifty in their use of water, fertilizer, and fresh soil, factors to which other plants—if they lack them—immediately respond with clear signals. In the case of cacti, we only notice that they are missing something when it is too late . . .

The Right Spot

Cacti will probably always favor the win-dow as "their" spot, for it makes no differ-ence whether the plants come from the high mountains of Central and South America or from the pampas in the south of the continent: They must always receive a maximum of light. For this reason, a win-dow with a northern exposure or one shaded by trees is not suitable for them. Thanks to their incredible adaptability, some especially tough varieties will man-age to stay alive, but we cannot expect good growth or even blooming.

Also, when placing cacti on the win-dowsill care should be taken to see that the plants always get fresh air—but no draft! The closer cacti are to the windowpane, the more care must be taken to see that there is adequate air circulation. A clear glass ter-rarium, close to the window, is also suitable for cacti. But here the supply of fresh air is just as important as the evaporation of water.

Accordingly, cacti need as much light as possible. Northern latitudes are not particu-larly favorable in this respect. Even on a

Bottom: These two trailing cacti are suit-able as hanging-basket plants in a bright window: *Aporocactus flagelli-formis* (top) and *Cleistocactus winteri* (bottom).

Page 16: An unheated greenhouse provides ideal conditions for the cactus collector.

A wide windowsill accommodates a considerable cactus collection.

TIP

I use a bowl with a large opening at the top as a terrarium, so that fresh air is present. The bottom layer of my potting mix is sand mixed with coarse gravel. That way I avoid the accumulation of moisture.

bright summer day, the intensity of light in northern regions is only about one-half that in the highlands of Mexico.

Added to this, northern regions also have rainy and overcast summer days. This is the main reason why some cacti will not bloom there and others will not develop such colorful spination as in their native habitat. There is also a difference between cities and rural areas, because solar radiation has a much greater effect out in the country than in urban areas. In the city, light is considerably more diffuse as a result of waste gases from traffic and industry. However, the sturdiness of cacti allows them to get along with little light, even if growth and development of the plants may not always be typical of the species. The more of a powdery bloom a cactus has, or the more hairy or spiny it is, the closer it can be placed to the window. The more leafy green it shows, the less suited it is for a window with a midday southern exposure. Cacti with a glaucous bloom have a

natural waxy protection against too much evaporation. Stoutly formed, ribbed cacti periodically provide their own shade.

During the summer most cacti can be left outdoors, where they have the necessary light and, above all, fresh air (see also page 37).

Caring for Your Cacti

Location

In most cases, it cannot be too hot for cacti in summer. It must be remembered, however, that light conditions and watering should be coordinated. This is the Alpha and Omega—as, incidentally, it is for all plants: A high temperature is of no use when plants are dry and in semi-darkness. Always try to keep a good balance!

In any case, young plants, seedlings, and freshly grafted or recently rooted cuttings need warmer conditions than older, hardened-off specimens. By the way, this also applies to winter quarters.

But even with their high heat requirements, we should not forget that cacti need lots of fresh air. For this reason, most of them are put into the garden or out on the balcony for the summer, even when nighttime temperatures get cooler. In any case, this is good for them, for then they develop resistance and will not fall prey to disease so quickly.

This great fresh-air requirement in cacti is important because this is how they balance their transpiration, which is kept to a minimum, and respiratory activity. Fresh air allows them to better absorb the necessary carbon dioxide from the air.

Watering

Even if cacti get too little rather than too much water, they must still be given abundant moisture in the main growing season. Eighty-five to ninety percent of the weight of a cactus consists of water. The body tissue of cacti is composed of relatively large but thin-walled cells. These have the primary task of storing water.

Although cacti are able to store water, they need to be given additional water during the summer (for winter bloomers, in the flowering season as well). Although a cactus does not immediately signal that it is "thirsty," naturally it grows much better when it is supplied with water. But one should only water again when the soil is completely dry—and then generously. Any excess water should be removed from the

saucer. Cacti rot easily, especially at the base of the stem; therefore, the plants should never be allowed to stand in water-logged soil. Most cacti are usually "watered to death!" In no case should they be kept constantly moist (exception: when propagating).

The ideal water to use for watering is good drinking water or rainwater, because most cacti prefer a slightly acidic range and

TIP

On cool nights I place young plants on a cork plate, in order to "keep their feet warm."

Cacti should be put outdoors for the summer, to harden them off; here we see *Opuntia* (center) and *Aporocactus* (on the right).

TIP

Water can be softened and made more acidic by hanging a small quantity of peat in a bag of cheesecloth in it overnight.

do not like hard water. Water hardness indicates the percentage of calcium and magnesium compounds in the water. Your local water supply department can give you this information.

After winter dormancy, begin watering cautiously, because the cacti must slowly readapt to summer conditions. But they quickly form fine fibrous roots again, which are able to absorb water and distribute it throughout the plant after only a few weeks. Never water a cactus directly on the plant body in the sun in summer! That results in unsightly burn marks, and hairy species develop dull yellow spots.

Soil and Fertilizing

Above all, cacti need a good porous potting medium. In other words, you can mix a little clean sand with standard potting soil and have the right soil for cactus. However, it is preferable to use soil that does not contain too much lime or too much nitrogen. Ready-made cactus soil, which is quite satisfactory for promoting good growth in our cacti, can also be purchased.

The same is true of fertilizing. Freshly grafted and newly repotted plants should not be fertilized at all. All other cacti may be fertilized, especially when they need humus (see the information in the descriptions starting on page 40), with a special cactus fertilizer—but only in summer!

Stop fertilizing in August, so that the plants will not send out new shoots but will go into their winter quarters with mature growth.

Repotting

As a rule, cacti are transplanted into fresh soil and a new container only once every two years. I have noticed one thing: Multiple-stemmed cacti must be repotted more frequently than single-column or globular cacti. I also repot the so-called leafy cacti *Epiphyllum* and *Schlumbergera* annually.

When repotting, the new container should be only a little larger than the old one. Cacti need a variety of containers and pots. Some are shallow-rooted and do well in flat dishes. Others have long taproots and need a deep and narrow pot. There are species, like most *Mammillaria,* that form thick cushions in clumps and should not be separated. Potting them separately would interfere with their unhampered growth. Cactus roots grow relatively slowly; for this reason, frequent repotting does them more harm than good.

To avoid injury, use gloves and tongs when repotting. Cacti with barbs, for

Gravel and sand in the bottom of the pot provide good drainage.

Top left: For better drainage, fill the bottom of the pot with crocks and gravel.

Top right: Before removing the plant from the old pot, loosen the roots carefully from the edge of the pot.

Center left and right: When removing the plant from the pot, be careful not to injure the roots; loosen the soil slightly with a stick.

Bottom left: When adding fresh potting mix, hold the cactus so that it gets fresh soil all around.

Bottom right: Then press down very carefully all around. Water after a day or two.

TIP

In order to remove the cactus easily from the old pot without damaging the roots, I stop watering for several days before repotting. In this way the old, dry soil can be shaken from the roots without injury to fine fibrous roots.

example, *Opuntia microdasys,* which are dismissed as fine bristles but which actually can cause purulent infections, are especially dangerous.

For repotting, I hold the cactus with a newspaper, packaging material, or a piece of cloth; that way I can hold the cactus firmly with one hand and maneuver easily with the other hand.

The pot with the cactus is carefully tapped all the way around on the edge of the table to loosen the soil. A few broken crocks are on the bottom of the new pot to aid in the drainage of water. A little gravel here also promotes drainage. Then I add just a little of the fresh mix, holding the plant in the center of the pot so that the rest of the soil can easily be added all around.

Never set the plant too deep, because cacti rot at the root neck. The soil around cacti should be pressed down just slightly. Newly repotted columnar cacti—climbing genera as well as *Selenicereus*—need a support. A frame or small trellis of bamboo or similar material stuck into the pot can be used for this.

Unlike other plants, cacti need not be watered immediately; they can be allowed to stand for a day or two and then watered. Newly repotted plants should be protected from drafts and kept warm and relatively moist.

Hydroponics

Most cacti will also grow well hydroponically. However, if you want to transplant cacti that have been grown in a soil mix into a hydroponic system, every bit of soil must be carefully washed out of the roots with a spray. Then the cacti can be potted in the new supporting medium.

In all of this, great care must be taken not to injure the roots. The supporting medium may be regular hydrogranules of clay; plastic beads or pebbles are also suitable. The important thing is for them to be free of pathogens and foreign substances and to provide the plant with sufficient support. No nutrient solution, but only plain water, is given for the first 14 days after repotting. Only then is a very weak fertilizer solution added, which can be made a little stronger after another two weeks. The water level should not be too high: otherwise the stems rot. The plants need no nutrient solution during the winter, and the potting medium should be kept only slightly moist.

Mammillaria zeilmanniana lends itself to hydroponic culture.

Propagating Your Own Cacti

Propagating cacti is not as complicated or as difficult as is often believed. As always with cacti, one need only have the necessary patience, because cacti do not grow as perceptibly fast as other plants.

Sowing Seed

This is the most common method of propagating cactus. However, it will be helpful first to check the chapter "A Selection of Beautiful Cacti" (see page 39 f.) for the corresponding genus, to see whether propagation by cuttings or later grafting leads to success more quickly.

The first thing needed is the seed in question, which can be obtained from dealers in the trade (see Sources of Supply, page 155). Of course, seeds that you harvest yourself can also be used. But then the pulp must be completely removed, or rot may develop. Absolute cleanliness is required in sowing seed—as in all other methods of propagation. A good time to start sowing is in April; that way the seedlings grow into the warm season.

A shallow pan or flat is used as a container. If several species are sown, the flat should be divided up by small wooden sticks right after being filled with soil—cacti are very hard to tell apart as seedlings. It is also advisable to have labels ready for marking.

The potting medium should consist mainly of clean sand and sifted cactus soil, with the proportion of sand twice that of the soil. For sowing, you may figure that an area of $\frac{1}{2}$—1 square inch (3–6 cm^2) has room for 10–20 seeds. Cactus seeds are very fine: therefore, the potting medium should be thoroughly moistened before sowing. This keeps the seeds from floating away. Do not cover the seeds with soil. Species of the

Large seeds like those of *Astrophytum* are pressed down to make contact with the soil. Do not cover with potting medium; cacti need light to germinate.

genera *Astrophytum* and *Frailea* germinate rapidly, after only three days. *Cereus* and *Opuntia* require a great deal of patience, because they often take a whole month to sprout.

Cactus seedlings need plenty of fresh air after sprouting.

TIP

Seedlings may
be protected
from strong
sunlight with
a sheet of
tissue paper or
newspaper.

Seedlings of
Mammillaria fittkaui,
which may now
be pricked out.
They bloom as
2-year-old plants.

The sown soil must always be kept moist; in no case should the germinating seeds be allowed to dry out or they will die. A favorable microclimate, therefore, is provided by laying a glass plate over the sown seeds. The temperature must always be 75 to 85°F (25 to 30°C). To prevent rotting, the seedlings should occasionally be ventilated by placing a little piece of wood between the plate and the flat. When the tiny plants bump up against the glass plate, it is time to remove the plate entirely.

Pricking Out

Meanwhile, plants will have become too tightly packed, so they must be pricked out. Pricking out is done to thin out the seedlings and should be performed very gently. The tiny delicate roots must not be injured. A flat or pot may again be used as the new container, but this time it should have drainage holes in the bottom. The potting medium can be a little richer in nutrients than the soil used for sowing.

For pricking out you need a pair of tweezers, which should not be too sharp-edged, and a transplanting fork. Grasp the seedling carefully with the tweezers and then slip the fork under the tiny plant. Lift the plant out of the sowing medium and place it in the transplanting soil, in which you have first made a hole. Select a distance that is one to two times the diameter of the seedlings. In order to prevent rotting, water only on the second day.

Now the little plants must be kept warm (71.6–77°F [22–25°C]), moist, and protected against drafts. Above all, they must be kept in bright light but without being exposed to the hot midday sun. Newly transplanted seedlings should be acclimated to the sun gradually. From time to time they also need fresh air.

If the plants get too crowded again, they should be pricked out a second time. During the winter the plants must not be allowed to fall below 50°F (10°C) and should be kept fairly dry. Usually the cacti develop so well that they can be put into separate pots in the spring.

Separating Pups—Taking Layers

Some cactus, e.g., *Mammillaria*, tend to form offshoots, which can be detached and used again as cuttings. These pups may also form roots right on the parent plant; then they can usually be removed very easily. If they are firmly attached, we use a sharp knife or razor blade to cut them off and allow them to dry in the air for a few days before they are placed in soil.

TIP

A transplanting fork is easy to make from a label, in which a small sharp cut is made at the narrow end.

Top: Using a pointed stick, the seedling is carefully lifted (left) and then removed from the potting medium with the fork (right).

Bottom: The stick is used to make a hole (left) before the plant is carefully set into it and soil gently pressed down around it (right).

Top right: Take cuttings only with an absolutely clean and very sharp knife.

Bottom right: Allow cut surfaces to dry in the air.

Bottom: Keep cuttings upright in the potting mix and do not move pots.

Propagation by Cuttings

Propagation by cuttings is done when the plants are "full of sap," that is, in the summer. This is a simple method of propagating cacti. Using a sharp, clean knife, make a straight horizontal cut through the plant. The level of the cut should be at the narrowest point of the cactus. The upper part will later become the new young plant.

In thicker shoots, the cut surface usually immediately curves inward. The new roots would then push through the cut at the lowest point, the outer skin. However, this would lead to one-sided, poor rootage; therefore, taper the cutting at the bottom,

without injuring the vascular bundle. In this way the roots are forced to break through the cut surface around the vascular bundle. Then we get strong, healthy roots.

The cuttings should not be allowed to sit for too long, or the roots will come out at the wrong place, namely on the areoles, which face downward when the cutting is lying on its side.

The top of the cutting will also always turn toward the light. This may result in misshapen plants. The best thing to do is just to put the cuttings into a well-ventilated, clean container after two days (without potting medium and without moisture). Full sun should be avoided until root formation.

As soon as the first root tips appear—as a rule, this takes 2–3 weeks—the cuttings are stuck down into the potting mix. Sand or a sand-and-cactus soil mixture has been found to be a good medium; the proportion of sand should be two-thirds. At temperatures of 68–77°F (20–25°C) the cuttings show, by new shoots and strong plant bodies, that they are rooting well.

Some cacti can be stimulated to form shoots by a cut on the main stem, and the shoots thus produced can be used later for propagation. However, this type of propagation detracts from the natural beauty of the parent plant.

Grafting

There are many species of cactus that grow very slowly on their own roots or that are hard to get to bloom. Here grafting is in order. But this should not become an addiction, with grafts being made willy-nilly. Species that grow and bloom well on their own roots should also be raised on their own roots, because this is more in accord with the natural conditions of cacti.

Poor growers or lazy bloomers are given a "growth booster" in the form of a rootstock. When grafted on a tall rootstock, some cacti grow twice as fast. And plants that are broken off, injured at the root neck, or diseased can still be saved in this way. There are also species and varieties, such as the colored forms of *Gymnocalycium mihanovichii* var. *friedrichii* (see page 84 f.),

that in temperate areas will grow only on grafted stock.

As in all methods of propagation, the best time for grafting is in the summer months, in dry and especially in warm weather. Fast-growing columnar cacti (e.g., *Cereus* or *Harrisia*) are suitable as rootstock; however, they should not form many side shoots.

The technical aids required are a thin and very sharp knife, a pair of tweezers, rubber bands, and a piece of cloth. The cut is begun at the point of the rootstock at which the previous year's fresh green stem begins. Cut horizontally through the rootstock, in approximately the upper third, pulling from the handle to the blade of the knife. When the stem is cut in two, sap must come out of the cut right away. If the cut surface immediately caves in, however, the rootstock should not be used. The upper rows of areoles of the

TIP

In order to be sure that the rootstock is strong enough, I place the plant selected for it in a warmer and brighter location three weeks in advance and feed it with a diluted fertilizing solution. It is also given ample water during this period.

Pups like this can simply be separated with a sharp knife and potted after they have dried out.

TIP

In order to prevent decay, I dust the cut surface with charcoal powder. You may also use sulfur powder.

Right: The vascular bundles, arranged in a ring, are clearly visible in this cut.

Far right: The edge of the scion is trimmed.

Bottom: The scion is fixed on the stock with two rubber bands.

stock may be trimmed off in order to prevent lateral growth. Then place the scion with its fresh surface, cut to fit exactly (when the stock has been trimmed, the scion should be cut wedge-shaped) on the stock so that the vascular bundles of the two cacti match up.

All this must be done very quickly and with the utmost cleanliness. Clean and dry the knife after every cut! It may also be dipped into an alcohol solution for disinfection.

The whole thing is fastened with rubber bands. First stretch a rubber band under the pot, then bring it up over the plant and carefully let it slide onto the scion. Use two rubber bands crosswise for each plant. The grafted plants are put in a dry and semi-shady location, protected from drafts, at about 75–85°F (25–30°C). The cut surfaces should not come into contact with water for the next two weeks. However, do not forget to water the stock, because it is already rooted.

Grafting of Seedlings

This method of propagation is quite special and requires greenhouse conditions, for the grafted plants must be kept at 85–95°F (30–35°C). In addition, the seedling is often too tiny and too soft for a regular rootstock. A small plate should be placed between the rubber band and the scion to prevent cutting in or flattening. The scions need something to hold them, for which plant labels may be used. Tips of *Selenicereus* and *Harrisia* are suitable as rootstocks. Later, feed with a very weak solution of fertilizer.

Cacti Get Sick

In general, cacti are very resistant to disease and pests. This is only partly true, however. Cacti do not react to cultural mistakes or diseases and pests as fast as other houseplants.

Usually damage is only noticed when it is too late. Nevertheless, the fact is that cacti are somewhat sturdier than soft-leaved houseplants. The Alpha and Omega of preventive plant protection is not to do anything seriously wrong—especially not over a long period of time. Application of basic information concerning the needs of cacti is usually enough, because a plant in harmony with its environment will seldom succumb to a pathogen. Weakened or debilitated plants, on the other hand, often have little chance of recovering from a heavy infestation. Added to this is another point that should not go unmentioned: Every living thing, hence every plant, gets used to its surroundings to some degree; it should come as no surprise, therefore, if a cactus that in winter was kept neither cool nor dry nevertheless comes into bloom.

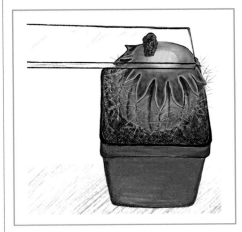

This only goes to show that, with cacti, we are dealing with variable living things and that it is up to us to be aware of the needs of each genus (see information in the descriptions starting on page 40) and so keep our plants strong and healthy. Since, as already mentioned, a disease does not suddenly break out in full force but its consequences only become apparent after some weeks, we should check our cacti very carefully every week.

(see information in the descriptions starting on page 40)

TIP

Lightly turning and pressing eliminates air bubbles on the cut surfaces.

Grafting Seedlings
Top: With a clean knife, a cut is made through the upper part of the rootstock, which has not yet become woody. The rings of areoles are trimmed off. The ring of vascular bundles of the rootstock is clearly visible.

Bottom: The seedling is so tiny that it is covered with a plate of glass for a little while, in order to prevent slipping. At the same time, the vessels of the vascular bundles of the two plants must be in contact with each other in at least one spot. This is the only way in which the scion can be maintained by the rootstock.

TIP

Our eye often fails to discover the dangerous webs, pathogens, or discolorations on the plant body. This is when a magnifying glass comes in handy.

TIP

Use a detergent to thoroughly clean places where cacti attacked by fungal disease have been kept.

Corking of the lower part of the plant, caused by growth disturbances among other things.

Cultural Mistakes

Often cultural mistakes are what first trigger a disease, but if they are corrected while the disease is in its initial stage they are remediable.

When cacti are kept warm and moist in winter, they form thin, light green stems that are clearly different from the rest of the plant body. If conditions that are right for the species are provided, the plant will go on to put out healthy growth again, but a thin central section will remain as a reminder of our mistake (see photograph on page 31).

Corking, especially at the base of cacti, may be a completely normal manifestation of age (e.g., *Opuntia*) or may be specific to the species, as in the case of *Echinopsis.* But temperature fluctuations, irregular watering, or an unfavorable winter location may also produce this phenomenon.

In order to defend themselves against such irregular conditions, plant tissues react with corking, laying down corky substances, known as suberins, in the cellulose layers of the cell walls. Thus, careful attention should always be paid to procedures for care and, in particular, the winter location.

The following should be noted, especially in the case of globular cacti growing cylindrically and in columnar cacti: Any disturbance of growth, including lack of moisture or nutritional deficiency but particularly too much moisture, lack of light, and extreme temperature fluctuations, is responded to by changes in the thickness of growth.

So-called **stem or root rots** often are only the consequence of too much moisture in the pot with simultaneous coolness, or of the plant being set too deeply in the soil. Fungi soon take hold under such unfavorable conditions.

Burn marks are quite a different signal, being evidence of intolerance to direct sun. Here light shading or a change of location will help. For example, the cactus should not be sprayed right when it is standing in the sun, because drops of water act like little burning glasses and intensify the effect of sunshine.

Lack of light leads to the same phenomena as too much warmth and humidity in winter: The color of the stems becomes light, almost yellowish, and the stems remain weak and thin. In their search for light they grow faster than otherwise and are very weak.

Lack of heat leads to interruptions in growth, if not to death of the entire plant, because then fungal pathogens can spread. Naturally, this does not happen if cacti get their winter rest, since growth processes slow down because everything—light, temperature, and moisture—is minimized and acts in equilibrium. Only when cold is accompanied by a great deal of moisture is damage inevitable.

Fungal Disease

Fungal disease generally can be recognized by the fuzzy gray coating at the top of plants. But rot, at the base of the stem and at the roots, is also the consequence of fungal infestation. Fungal disease often spreads in seed flats, because sufficient moisture is available there. Here only careful removal of the

Top: Lack of light in *Mammillaria,* at left in photograph; at right, a healthy plant.

Bottom: In columnar cacti, lack of light results in thin tips, which become a normal size when light is provided.

At right: Cactus seedlings with severe fungal disease.

Far right: Rotted vascular bundles.

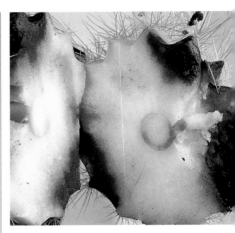

Bottom: This globular cactus evidently stayed cool and especially too wet for too long, and can no longer be saved.

islands of fungi involved, constant inspection, and ventilation will help.

Fungal masses must be removed very carefully, since they reproduce through countless, barely visible spores that fly away easily. Larger cacti can be saved by making a sharp cut in healthy tissue and grafting the plant body (see page 27 ff.).

Lack of good air circulation is usually the reason for the appearance of fungal disease, but too much water or too little warmth may also be reasons. Accordingly, one of the most important steps to take is to quickly check cultural conditions and make any necessary changes. Measure temperature with a thermometer, not by how you feel; check moisture by removing the root ball from the pot, not by sticking your finger into the soil. A rotten odor of the soil is a sign of overwatering.

In addition, ask yourself: When did I last give this plant a good airing?

Pests
Various species of aphids head the list of

nsect pests. Sometimes the plant bodies urn yellowish, shrivel up, and stop growng. Then woolly aphids and mealybugs nay be the cause. They can be recognized by their white woolly webs, in which the eggs of the woolly aphid are found. Hardto-reach places, for example, between areoles, in the interfaces of grafted cacti, in the axils of leafy cactus, or between parent cactus and pup, tend to get coated. The brown-gray insects pierce the plants and suck out their sap. They appear especially when cacti are kept too warm and in air that is too dry in winter.

The first thing, if possible, is to pick off the insects and paint their remaining nests with a brush dipped in cooking oil. This smothers the eggs and the insects. After that, carefully wash off the affected cactus with a weak detergent solution. During all of these operations, always be sure to cover the soil carefully with foil, so that no insects can get into it.

Ants in cacti are often an indication of **aphids,** for the two enter into a symbiosis: The ants feed on so-called honeydew, a sticky secretion excreted by aphids. This is frequently observed on young stems. The infested spot exhibits traces of feeding, at which the edges are crusted. Aphids can be washed off easily with a strong lukewarm stream of water.

Similar webs often found on the roots come from root mealybugs. These are discovered when the plant is taken out of the pot. To get rid of these, the old soil is completely removed. A hose is used to wash away the last bits of soil. Now the cactus is potted into fresh soil. Use an absolutely clean pot here! If there are several plants in a dish, all of them should be cleaned and repotted, even if only one plant seems to be infested.

TIP

Before potting, I dip the cleaned roots into a weak soapy solution.

Top: Woolly aphids and mealybugs are easy to recognize but hard to remove, because they settle into the recesses of the plant.

Center: Aphids first attack the delicate parts of the plant, like the buds of *Epiphyllum* here.

Bottom: Root mealybugs have spread throughout the soil and onto the roots.

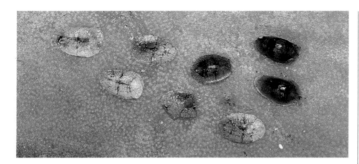

Top: Scale insects can be removed, but the soil in the pot must be covered.

Bottom: Red spiders produce a picture of damage that looks like the result of cultural mistakes. Because of that, the real cause is usually discovered too late.

Everything must be done very carefully, because root mealybugs develop rootlike waxy webs, which can easily be mistaken for fine fibrous roots that should not be disturbed.

Scale insects are also frequently found on cacti. They have a special preference for columnar and rock cacti. The young insects or eggs lie under roundish brown scales. The best thing to do is to pick these all off. But be sure to cover the soil, because otherwise the insects simply drop off and are soon found on the plant again. After removing them, wash off the cactus carefully with a weak detergent solution. Scale infestation often results in bud and shoot drop. Even the deep green of the cactus body suffers: Plants develop a yellowish appearance.

Now and then **ants** may cause trouble in a collection, especially when they make their nest right in the cactus pots. In addition, they have a great fondness for grains of seed from ripening fruits. Even a single ant should be removed immediately, because it gnaws at the stamens of the flowers.

Dangerous **spider mites** are known by the name **"red spider."** These are some of the most harmful of cactus pests, because they are usually not noticed until it is too late. The insects are so tiny (barely 1 mm) that they can only be definitely detected with a magnifying glass. The damage that they do is easier to see: grayish brown, yellowish, and later brown spots that spread. These insects are very active, especially around the top of the plant. The tiny (0.25–0.5 mm) reddish spiders sit in a web of fine whitish filaments and suck plant sap. This results in damage due to drying. Here only a chemical insecticide will help. If cacti are kept in extremely dry indoor air for a long time, they can easily become infested with spider mites. Affected plants must be isolated promptly.

Snails and **slugs** are not likely to appear indoors, but they may easily be brought in from summer garden quarters. Before bringing in your plants, therefore, examine pots and plants for their typical slimy tracks and then remove the slugs. Even densely spined cacti may be affected. Usually the undersides of pots are the place where slugs are found. So look for them there, because their chomping causes great damage.

TIP

Echinopsis chamaecereus is a so-called spider mite herald, since it is extremely susceptible to this pest. If it has no spider mites, none of the other cacti in the collection will be infested either.

Cacti in Winter

Most cacti must have a bright, very cool, and dry place in winter. They need this rest or dormant period, in which they do not grow, to set buds for the next year. Studies have shown that there must be a dormant period of at least 40 to 70 days. With the increasing duration of this dormant period the number of flowers formed also increases. Induction of flowering likewise requires ample light in the winter quarters, as well as in the early spring location. When plants are watered too early and too generously in the spring, slumbering flower buds may atrophy.

The large majority of cacti are best overwintered at 40–50°F (5–10°C). *Rebutia* may be kept even cooler, but should not be exposed to frost. These are only guidelines, however. Cacti are relatively tough and also survive brief periods of much higher or lower temperatures without appreciable damage.

To protect cacti from especially cold frosty nights, a piece of cardboard can be slipped between the plants and the windowpane. In no case should the plant body be allowed to touch the glass.

During the dormant period, cacti should be watered just enough to keep them alive. A few drops every week are sufficient. One need not worry about shriveling of the plants. As soon as the cactus gets light, warmth, and moisture again, its plant body firms up. During the winter it draws on the reserves of water and nutrients that it has stored in its tissues.

Adequate light in the winter quarters is important, not only because otherwise cacti will have fewer flowers, but because their growth suffers from lack of light. Since we cannot provide cacti with much light anyway—compared to their native habitats—they react especially sensitively to dark places in winter. They put out long, thin growth, known as "etiolation." Columnar cacti lose their compact harmonious shape. They develop thin tips, which are then followed by thicker growth again in the summer. Globular cacti do not remain spheres but form distinctly slenderer shapes. All of this is only the plant's reaction to its desperate search for light: It stretches itself toward the little that we offer it with increased longitudinal growth.

Just as important as providing light is ventilating the plants' winter quarters once every week. Naturally, this should not be done on a day when the weather is freezing, because ice cold air should be kept from striking the unprepared plants directly. A thick layer of newspaper serves as good protection.

TIP

I usually water flowering cacti only when I see the first buds.

These flowering plants obviously had an optimum winter location.

Through the Year with Cacti

Echinopsis aurea appreciates regular spraying in summer.

Small heavily spined cacti can be repotted using barbecue tongs.

January

Winter quarters should definitely be ventilated on clear days. But take care, because at very low temperatures the cold air may damage plants. So this is my tip: Use a thick newspaper to protect cacti from penetrating cold air on windowsills.

If some cacti already show bud set, they may be placed in a slightly warmer spot and gradually be given more moisture.

If cacti are kept in the basement, look underneath the pots for sow bugs and slugs and remove them.

If the place where cacti are overwintered is very dark, be sure to provide additional light for several hours a day.

February

Even if the sun shines more brightly now, plants should not be watered more heavily. If the cacti are standing directly on the windowsill, they can be lightly shaded from strong sunshine with a sheet of tissue paper: otherwise, growth processes will start too early and be one-sided. Temperatures must not be allowed to get too high, no more than 60°F (15°C) on the average. Therefore ventilate more often. In doing so, be sure to avoid drafts. Now that *Epiphyllum* is growing again, water a little more generously.

Be sure to inspect the cacti for pests. This is also the time to set up a cactus file in which to record the development of your spiny plants.

March

Gradually remove the cacti from their winter quarters. They should be dusted off or sprayed.

Do these tasks so that the plants are dried off by nighttime: otherwise, rot and fungus may develop. Never spray plants in the sun! This results in burn marks. The cacti now need lots of light and ample moisture. Still, they should be protected from strong sun. Light shade is advisable, or the plants will be damaged. When the first cacti produce their flowers, feed them with a special cactus fertilizer. Now the other cacti may be lightly fertilized for the first time, too.

April

Repotting season begins. Cacti that already have buds or are in bloom, however, are only repotted after flowering. The plants should now be kept warm again and given plenty of light and regular watering. Fertilize plants that are in bloom once a week. The first seeds may be sown. Be sure not to forget identifying labels, because cactus seedlings all look alike. Cacti with few spines are not yet exposed to full sun but are lightly shaded. Sturdy older plants can now be put outdoors for several hours. But be careful; don't forget to bring them in for the night! There may still be damaging frosty nights.

May

Most cacti are now blooming in all their splendor. They can be pollinated with a fine brush. Propagation by cuttings should be done now, and this month is also favorable for grafting, because rootstocks are full of sap and are growing.

Seedlings in flats can be pricked out for the first time. Although it cannot be too warm for most genera, do not forget that cacti that are placed directly in a south-facing window need good air circulation. Less sensitive cacti like *Opuntia, Cereus,* and *Echinopsis* can now stay outdoors in light shade all day long.

This is also a good time to shift cacti from soil to a hydroponic culture.

June

Be sure to take newly acquired plants out of their pots and examine them for root mealy-bugs. If necessary, keep them away from other plants and treat them as required!

Cacti need fresh air at night, too. Temperature differences between day and night are optimal for cacti this month. Water heavily during the day; as a rule of thumb, this may be done once to twice a week. A shower is good for the plants, too. But not in the sun—that would result in burn marks! And watering can be skipped on cool and cloudy days. Cacti that have not yet been repotted can now be placed in fresh soil. However, do not fertilize. Grafting may also be continued. Shade seedling grafts lightly with tissue paper.

July

Beautifully and densely haired cacti should not be put outdoors, because the air is often very dusty during these months. Other cacti do very well outdoors. But not all of them tolerate full sun. For example, leafy cacti should also be placed in the shade outdoors. Be careful about slugs. Set pots in dry saw-dust, sand, or pine bark mulch.

By now most cacti are out in full sun and heat. But caution is in order: Overheating of cacti can be avoided by providing abundant ventilation and light shade. Water generously and do not forget to spray, but never do this in strong sun.

The plants may also be fed with a special cactus fertilizer in liquid form.

August

The cacti have gotten used to full sun, so that sun-loving genera need no longer be shaded. Leafy cacti and other shade-loving cacti should not be kept in full sun.

This is the month in which the cacti are fertilized for the last time. No more repotting should be done either, except for those plants that were pricked out in the spring and so are now getting their own pots. Plants must be mature when they go into winter dormancy.

However, cacti may still be propagated by cuttings.

In order to harden them off, the plants should purposely be exposed to temperature fluctuations between day and night.

Cut down a little on watering now. Pay special attention to spider mite infestation around this time of year.

Aporocactus flagelli-formis also does well outdoors during the summer.

TIP

To keep slugs away, I put a dish with beer in it alongside my cacti when they go out-doors.

Rhipsalis makes berrylike fruits, the seeds of which can be used for sowing.

Page 39: *Epiphyllum chrysocardium*

TIP

TIP

So that frosty air will not damage my cacti, I cover them with thick paper before ventilating them.

September

This is the time to prepare your winter quarters: Clean, disinfect if necessary, and make sure you have thick windowpanes. The plants now get watered less frequently, are no longer fertilized, and get plenty of fresh air even at night; this increases their resistance.

Examine outdoor plants for infestations of all kinds.

Keep *Schlumbergera truncata* relatively dry for about four weeks from mid-September on (although stems should not shrivel!); keep it very cool and in bright light and then this Christmas cactus will set lots of flower buds. No more propagating now.

October

Outdoor *Opuntias* may be covered. Suitable materials are brushwood, straw, or pine bark mulch.

The cacti now should be gradually moved into their winter quarters. They continue to need ample light at this time. But watering is almost completely halted. If the plants are kept warm, they still need some watering. Because of early night frosts, the cacti can be ventilated only during the day. However, this should be done without fail, to harden them off.

Winter bloomers, like *Rhapsalis* and *Schlumbergera,* should now be kept warmer and moister.

The few cacti that are still outdoors should be protected from rain.

Nutrient solutions should be removed from hydroponic systems and cacti placed in their winter quarters with a little plain water.

November

Winter quarters should be bright; a dark place is always only a temporary expedient. And cacti removed from their pots and wrapped in newspaper should be the exception. On average, favorable temperatures are between 40 and about 55°F (5 and 12°C)—always check the thermometer.

When night frosts are expected, slip a piece of cardboard between the plants and the windowpane for safety's sake.

All propagating should be left for spring.

If part of a cactus must be cut off for special health reasons, it should be allowed to dry in a cool (55°F [13°C]) and well-ventilated location until spring and not be grafted or used as a cutting until then.

December

Additional light can now be provided for several hours a day in winter quarters. The temperature should be checked regularly. Pay attention to weather reports, in order to cushion the effect of possible heavy night frosts by covering with paper.

Winter-blooming plants are kept ventilated and warmer, and are watered regularly.

Cactus potting mixes—including those for hydroponic plants—are moistened slightly every two weeks. Ventilate winter quarters in clear (not damp) weather; however, protect cacti from sudden drafts of cold air.

Inspect all cacti regularly for pests, and isolate infested plants; spider mites and woolly aphids can easily sneak in.

A Selection of Beautiful Cacti

TIP

I only water these plants with rainwater.

Acanthocalycium glaucum

Acanthocalycium violaceum

Acanthocalycium

Origin This beautiful flowering cactus comes from Argentina. The cactus specialist C. Backeberg described it in 1930. Older sources place it in the genera *Echinopsis, Helianthocereus,* and *Lobivia.*

Care *Acanthocalycium* grows in acidic soil. Use only lime-free fertilizer when fertilizing in summer. The plant is not demanding and blooms readily if it is kept relatively dry and at a temperature of no more than 30°F (−1.1°C) in winter.

Propagation Propagation is from seed.

Species *A. glaucum* is globular in shape, with blue-gray and black spines. The large flowers are golden yellow.

A. hyalacanthum grows up to 14 inches (35 cm) high and 4 inches (10 cm) in diameter. Its whole exterior looks gray, because the plant body and the areoles are grayish green. The spines are whitish and point downward. The large flowers are also white.

A. peitscherianum is flattened-globular, becoming at most 3 inches (8 cm) high and 4 inches (10 cm) broad. The flowers grow 2¼ inches (6 cm) long and are a pale lilac-pink. They have brownish scale leaves.

As a young plant, *A. spiniflorum* is globular; later it grows up to 2 feet (60 cm) high and resembles a cylinder. The light yellow flowers grow up to 2 inches (5 cm) wide.

A. violaceum bears light violet, funnel-shaped flowers of up to 2¾ inches (7 cm). The plant body is globular and has a diameter of about 5 inches (13 cm). When it is older, it lengthens. The areoles are white, the spines pale yellow.

Aporocactus
Rat-tail Cactus

Origin This thin-stemmed cactus is native to central Mexico. It was described for the first time in 1860 by the French cactus expert A. C. Lemaire. Several species were formerly included in the genus *Cereus.*

Habit As the name itself suggests, *Aporocactus* is a creeping or trailing tree-dweller (epiphyte) with strong aerial roots and stems about 4¾ inches (12 cm) long, which get no thicker than 1¼ inches (3 cm). It is densely covered with short yellowish or brownish spines.

Care *Aporocactus* needs a soil rich in humus. To prevent red spider and other mites, high humidity should be provided during the summer by spraying. A bright location is necessary: otherwise, the intensity of flower color diminishes.

Propagation Propagation is by cuttings.

Species **A. conzatti** has brick-red flowers.

A. flagelliformis has 3-inch (8-cm) crimson flowers that last for several days.

A. martianus has pink flowers. The stems are barely ¾ inch (2 cm) thick; the spines are bristlelike.

A. mallisonii is a cross between *A. flagelliformis* and *Heliocereus speciosus;* it looks very much like the former but has thicker stems. It was first seen in bloom in London in 1832.

Aporocactus flagelliformis

Aporocactus mallisonii

TIP

This cactus can also be grown hydroponically.

Ariocarpus agavoides

Ariocarpus fissuratus

Ariocarpus retusus

Ariocarpus
Living Rock Cactus

Origin This interesting and rare cactus comes from the northeast of Mexico. It was discovered there at an altitude of 3,900 feet (1,200 m) in limestone mountains. It is often still classified under the genera *Neogomesia* and *Roseocactus*. This genus was established by M. J. E. Scheidweiler (1799–1861), professor of botany at the Institut Horticole in Ghent.

Habit This broad, round, domed cactus has a thick taproot that enables it to survive extreme dry periods, because the root serves as a water reservoir. It has greatly elongated tubercles, which are arranged in spirals. The plant body is bluish green. It has no spines. The flowers emerge from dense axillary wool and bloom for only a day.

Care This cactus needs a soil rich in lime, to which some loam may be added. In its dormant period, which is in the summer months in northern climates, the cactus should be kept warm but almost completely dry. *Ariocarpus* is a short-day plant; its principal growing season is in the fall.

With the exception of *A. retusus,* watering can begin again cautiously in August. The watering period lasts into November.

This genus grows very slowly on its own roots and is also hard to maintain. Grafted plants are less sensitive.

Propagation Propagation is from seed.

Species *A. agavoides* has flowers that are white on the outside and pink in the center.

A. fissuratus has pink flowers with dark stripes in the center.

A. kotschoubeyanus (Edelweiss Cactus) is only 2 inches (5 cm) in size and has pink to dark red flowers that are almost as big.

A. retusus is probably the most robust species. The flowers are pale pink to white. This species should be watered starting in September.

A. scaphorostrus is broad-round and has stunning violet flowers.

A. trigonus often gets its yellowish-white flowers all at the same time and, therefore, is especially attractive when in bloom. Its principal growing season is in the fall.

TIP

Be wary of spider mites; they like to settle on *Ariocarpus*.

Ariocarpus trigonus

Ariocarpus scaphorostrus

INFO

This species was named in honor of Dr. Miguel Arrojado, who, as head of the Brazilian railroad, made possible the exploration of an especially difficult area, the caatinga (thornbush region). This cactus was found there.

Arrojadoa penicillata

Astrophytum myriostigma

Arrojadoa penicillata

Origin This columnar cactus comes from Brazil. *Arrojadoa* was described by two cactus scholars, N. Lord Britton (1859–1934) and J. N. Rose (1862–1928).

Habit This cactus is slender and has multiple stems. It forms a shrub up to 6½ feet (2 m) high. A dense, bristly cephalium, from which the night-blooming flowers appear, is found at the top. The cephalia, which also produce the young shoots, look like ruffs. The reddish flowers open wide in the early morning.

Care *Arrojadoa* likes a slightly acidic soil, rich in humus. It should not be placed in strong sun in the summer; in winter, the temperature should not go below 32°F (0°C).

Propagation Propagation is from seed.

Other Species **A. rhodantha** has rose-pink flowers and dark brown spines.

Astrophytum
Bishop's Cap, Star Cactus

Origin *Astrophytum* is found in the hot hillside areas of Central America. This attractive genus was described by the French cactus authority A. C. Lemaire (1800–1871).

Habit The genus *Astrophytum* varies greatly in appearance. Some species are devoid of spines; others have curved or stiff long spines.

The plant bodies are generally flattened-globular and have white flecks on the surface. The large yellow flowers, some with a red throat, appear in the center of the crown.

Care Since *Astrophytum* comes from warm south Texas and northern Mexico, these species are more sensitive to moisture in summer than other cacti, so never overwater them. These plants need a sunny location. The soil should be slightly acidic and consist of a mixture of special cactus soil and gravel. I always sprinkle some fine sand on the surface—especially on the root neck—in order to avoid moisture on the body of the plant. *Astrophytum* is kept almost dry in winter, when temperatures should be around 30°F (−1.1°C). *Astrophytum* is a sure bloomer if these few cultural hints are followed.

Propagation Propagation is from seed. However, since all astrophytes are sensitive to moisture, a so-called seedling graft is recommended. Seedlings are grafted on healthy rootstocks of *Echinopsis,* giving them an excellent start. After a few years they can be cut off again and rooted.

Species *A. asterias* (Sea Urchin Cactus) is a striking flat-growing cactus without spines. The white flecks on the smooth, green body of the plant are eye-catching. The flowers are yellow with a reddish center.

Astrophytum capricorne

INFO

The naturalist W. Karwinsky von Karwin (1780–1855) sent *Astrophytum asterias* to Europe for the first time in 1843. One specimen went to Munich, another to St. Petersburg. But nowhere was propagation successful. Not until 80 years later was this species propagated on the Continent, thanks to a discovery by the Czech cactus authority A. V. Frič.

Top:
Astropytum asterias

Astrophytum ornatum

A. capricorne has twisting bristles and magnificent 2¾-inch (7-cm) flowers with a bright red throat. *A. capricorne* is globular when young and only becomes somewhat columnar when mature. Its ribs have sharp edges. The dark green plant body is flecked with white.

A. myriostigma, the Bishop's Cap, has a rotund, slightly speckled body that is completely spineless and actually does resemble a bishop's miter in appearance. The flowers open when the sun shines and close up again in the evening.

A. ornatum: When young, this species is globular; when mature, the plant may develop into a column 3 feet (1 m) high. It has short, hard spines; its yellow flowers are funnel-shaped. It is also known as the "showy" *Astrophytum.*

Austrocephalocereus dybowskii

Origin This species is native to the northeast of Brazil. The genus was given its name by the German cactus specialist C. Backeberg (1894–1966).

Habit This columnar cactus is striking for its beautiful spination, the effect of which is heightened by the dense hairy covering. Yellow-white flowers emerge directly from the cephalium. They appear at dusk and open up fully at night.

A. dybowskii can grow up to 13 feet (4 m) high and branches at its base.

Care *Astrocephalocereus* is not sensitive to moisture and may be kept outdoors during the summer. Loamy cactus soil should be used as the growing medium. In winter this cactus should be kept a little warmer than other cacti; the temperature should never be allowed to go below 32°F (0°C).

Propagation Propagation is from seed.

Other Species *A. purpureus* has red flowers.

Austrocephalocereus dybowskii

Aztekium ritteri

Origin This curious genus comes from Mexico. It was first described by the German craftsman and cactus student F. Bödecker (1867–1937).

Habit The ribbed folds of the small rotund cactus are reminiscent of the writing of the Aztecs—hence the name. *Aztekium* has a gray body. Sometimes offshoots are formed. The small white flowers are trumpet-shaped.

Care *Aztekium* must have plenty of sun during the summer. Don't overwater! Regular cactus soil without anything added is satisfactory as the growing medium. In winter the plant should be kept cool, in the light, and relatively dry.

Propagation Propagation is from seed and by grafting of cuttings.

Other Species C. Backeberg speculated that there is another form with large flowers.

Aztekium ritteri

Top: *Blossfeldia liliputana*

TIP

Sprinkling some sand on the surface of the soil for Blossfeldia promotes water drainage.

Browningia hertlingiana

Blossfeldia liliputana

Origin This dwarf cactus is native to the north of Argentina and the south of Bolivia. The cactus specialist E. Werdermann (1892–1959) named this genus in honor of H. Blossfeld (born 1913), the German botanist and cactus authority.

Habit These tiny cacti flower at a plant diameter of less than ½ inch (1 cm), growing no bigger than ⅗ inch (1.5 cm). With its many off-shoots, *Blossfeldia* forms dense clusters. Spines and ribs are absent. The white flowers are very small and are borne on attractive stems.

Care *Blossfeldia* must have a sunny place all summer long. Use a potting mix that contains gravel and water sparingly, or you run the risk of rot.

Propagation Propagation is from seed.

Browningia hertlingiana

Origin Specimens 33 feet (10 m) tall of this magnificent, bluish columnar cactus are found in the dry valleys of Peru. It was described by the Austrian botanist F. Buxbaum (1900–1979). The genus has also been labeled *Azureocereus, Castellanosia, Cereus, Clistanthocereus, Gymnocereus,* and *Gymnanthocereus.*

Habit The white scaly flowers, which open at night, are delicately scented.

Care *Browningia* tolerates full sun; when kept in the shade, it loses its glaucous bloom. In summer, water only after the soil has dried out completely. Do not spray.

Propagation Propagation is from seed.

Other Species *B. chlorocarpa* bears red flowers, while *B. microsperma* has white flowers. The flowers of *B. viridis* are green.

Carnegiea
Saguaro Cactus

Origin *Carnegiea* is found in the United States (Arizona, California) and Mexico. This genus was described by the botanists N. Lord Britton (1859–1934), director of the New York Botanical Garden, and J. N. Rose (1862–1928), botanist at the United States National Herbarium.

Habit These giant columnar cacti grow 50 feet (15.2 m) high, and develop branches when mature. Their horny spines are arranged radially. The flowers are around 4¾ inches (12 cm), produced in large numbers, and last until the following day. Their delicate scent attracts the moths that pollinate them.

Care The saguaro never gets as big in cultivation as it does in the wild. Nevertheless, it is a beautiful columnar cactus. Use regular cactus soil as potting mix. Provide drainage with crocks and added gravel, since *Carnegiea* is sensitive to waterlogging. In the summer it needs a bright and airy location but should not stand in full sun. During the winter it should be kept relatively dry at 30°F (–1.1°C); at the same time, it is important for it to get enough light.

Propagation Propagation is from seed.

Species *C. gigantea* (formerly also known as *Cereus giganteus*) has white flowers. *C. polylophia* (previously listed under the genus *Neobuxbaumia*) has red flowers.

Carnegiea gigantea

Carnegiea polylopha

INFO

The flower of *Carnegiea gigantea* is the state flower of Arizona. These gigantic cacti can live to be more than 250 years old.

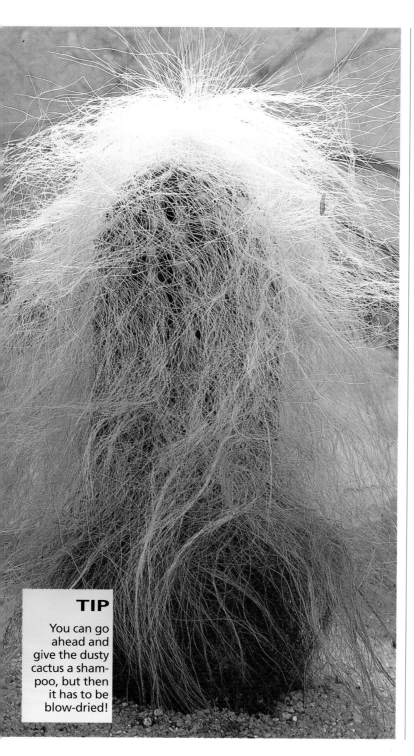

TIP

You can go ahead and give the dusty cactus a shampoo, but then it has to be blow-dried!

Cephalocereus senilis
Old Man Cactus

Origin This beautiful columnar cactus comes from Mexico. The genus was described by the German physician and botanist L. G. K. Pfeiffer (1805–1877). Many species that are now included under the genera *Austrocephalocereus*, *Espostoa*, *Micranthocereus*, *Pilosocereus*, and *Stephanocereus* were formerly listed under *Cephalocereus*. Today many botanists view *C. senilis* as the sole species of the genus. Previously it was also known as *Pilocereus senilis.*

Habit Its appearance is unmatched: A heavy, white fuzzy coat of hair makes *Cephalocereus* one of the most striking columnar cacti. It can grow up to 49 feet (15 m) high. The interesting thing about the Old Man Cactus is the cephalium, which surrounds it completely from a height of 20 feet (6 m). The pale yellow flowers, on the other hand, are inconspicuous.

Care In summer, *C. senilis* needs two weeks of dormancy, during which it must be dry. In winter, too, it should be kept relatively dry at about 32°F (0°C). In any case, it should only be watered from the bottom, so that no water gets onto the woolly coat of hair. Cover the soil with a layer of sand, to prevent waterlogging.

Propagation Propagation is from seed.

Cephalocereus senilis

Cereus
Torch Cactus

Origin All species of Cereus come from South America. The genus was described by the British botanist P. Miller (1691–1771). Today some species of *Cereus* are found in other genera, e.g., *Aporocactus, Browningia, Cleistocactus, Clistanthocereus, Corryocactus, Haageocereus, Monvillea, Peniocereus, Piptanthocereus, Polaskia, Praecereus, Selenicereus, Stenocereus, Stetsonia,* and *Subpilocereus.*

Habit *Cereus* is **the** columnar cactus par excellence, although this genus, with a large number of species, contains representatives of many different shapes. The flowers usually have long tubes and are not very scaly. As a rule, the stem is a lush green or blue-green.

Care *Cereus* likes an open and airy location in summer. In winter it must be kept cool and dry. Give it a planting mix rich in nutrients, with soil containing loam and gravel. This genus is relatively insensitive to waterlogging. *Cereus* is a fast-growing cactus and, therefore, a favorite for use as a rootstock in grafts.

Cereus huntingtonianus

Cereus jamacaru
'Monstrosus'

Cereus peruvianus
'Monstrosus'

Species *C. huntingtonianus* does not bloom until it is quite old. The white flowers open at night and fade in the course of the next day. The large funnel-shaped flowers are covered with scales on the outside, and are not hairy or spiny, as many sources incorrectly report. This species probably comes from Argentina.

C. jamacaru is a treelike cactus with a large crown. It comes from Brazil. The stems are a lush green, the spines yellow-brown. *C. jamacaru* has 10-inch (25-cm) white flowers. The well-known 'Monstrosus' variety is irregularly shaped.

C. peruvianus 'Monstrosus' has been known as a variety since the 18th century. It is the typical rock cactus. South America is assumed to be its homeland. The short, reddish-brown spines are set on the curious plant body in thick clusters. Its flowers are white.

C. aethiops bears pale pink flowers and is a native of Argentina.

C. alacriportanus has yellowish-pink flowers and comes from South America.

The Brazilian *C. azureus* has a glaucous bloom.

The "steel-blue" *Cereus,* however, is *C. chalybaeus* from South America.

The Argentine *C. dayamii* has funnel-shaped white flowers.

The white-flowered *C. hexagonus* is equipped with 6 ribs.

C. neotetragonus bears pinkish-red blossoms.

C. stenogonus, which ranges from Bolivia to Paraguay and Argentina, has a narrow-ribbed body.

Cleistocactus

Origin This genus of cactus, containing many species, is found from Peru through Bolivia to Argentina, Paraguay, and Uruguay. It is often found as a column or shrub at altitudes of 5,700 feet (1,750 m) in the mountains. The genus was described by the French cactus specialist A. C. Lemaire (1800–1871). Many species were formerly listed under the genera *Akersia, Borzicactella, Borzicactus, Bolivicereus, Cephalocleistocactus, Cereus, Denmoza, Hildewintera, Loxanthocereus, Matucana, Oreocereus, Seticereus, Seticleistocactus, Wintera,* and *Winterocereus.*

Habit Some species form magnificent columns, while others grow as treelike shrubs or even creep as ground covers. These slender-stemmed cacti branch at the base and form new branches on the sides. The bristles are thin, sometimes actually hairy, occasionally dense, rarely sparse. The cylindrical flowers are produced in shades of red, orange, yellow, or white. There are some species that—usually in maturity—bloom exceptionally profusely.

Care In summer *Cleistocactus* prefers a warm, generally sunny location and generous watering. The potting medium should be enriched with a little humus. In winter this cactus should be given bright light and kept dry at about 32°F (0°C). If kept warmer, it must also be given more water. *Cleistocactus* is eminently suited to being grown hydroponically, since it is not sensitive to moisture.

Cleistocactus ritteri

TIP

Cleistocactus will grow much better when a little crushed brick is mixed into the potting medium.

Cleistocactus strausii

Propagation Propagation is from seed and by cuttings, which should first be left out in the air to dry.

Species *C. candelilla* is also called Little Candelabra Cactus. It grows in columnar form and reaches a height of 3 feet (1 m). The yellow flowers have brown tips.

C. icosagonus usually grows erect, but sometimes it also creeps. The spines are a brilliant golden yellow.

C. ritteri has slightly curved, lemon-yellow flowers and green stigmas. It grows 3 feet (1 m) high and branches from below. The stems are very slender, having a diameter of only a little more than one inch (3 cm).

C. samaipatanus is an especially attractive species. It forms clusters, grows up to 5 feet (1.50 m) high, and branches heavily. The

Cleistocactus winteri

flowers are deep red and have long, dark red filaments.

C. strausii is probably the best known *Cleistocactus* species. The white bristles of the "Silver Torch" form a thick hairy coating. The narrow flower tubes are wine red, but are produced only in older specimens.

C. winterii was formerly called *Hildewintera aureispina.* The yellow spines cover the whole plant and make it very attractive even without flowers. The stems grow 5 feet (1.50 m) long and bend downward. This species, therefore, makes a very suitable hanging-basket plant (see photograph on page 17). The flowers are bright orange and last for several days.

Other Species Some examples of other species are *C. acanthurus, C. anguinus, C. areolatus, C. baumannii, C. brookei, C. roezlii,* and *C. sepium.*

Right: *Cleistocactus samaipatanus*

Bottom: *Cleistocactus icosagonus*

TIP

Copiapoa likes light shade, so I don't keep the plants right in the window during summer.

Copiapoa cinerea

Copiapoa coquimbana

Copiapoa cinerea

Origin This plant comes from Chile. *Copiapoa* was named in 1922 by the botanists N. Lord Britton (1859–1934) and J. N. Rose (1862–1928) for the Chilean city of Copiapo. Formerly it was also known under the name *Pilocopiapoa*.

Habit These cacti, at first globular, later become columnar. Their outer skin is exceptionally firm. The body of *C. cinerea* has an ash-gray bloom, with black spines. *Copiapoa* generally forms offshoots. Its sometimes scented flowers are light yellow to yellow.

Care The unusual thing about *Copiapoa* is that its *principal growing season* is in the fall. It should, therefore, be kept dry for a while in summer. But *Copiapoa* should stay in the light and be kept cool (around 32°F [0°C]) and dry in winter as well. Regular cactus soil is satisfactory.

Propagation Propagation is from seed and by grafting.

Other Species *C. cineracens* is ash-gray and has yellow flowers with recurved sepals.

C. coquimbana is a clustering species that has bell-shaped yellow flowers. *C. echinoides* is hedgehoglike, with pale yellow flowers and reddish sepals, while yellow-flowering *C. haseltoniana* branches from the base.

C. krainziana has white bristles and yellow blossoms with red margins. *C. pepiniana* bears yellow flowers.

C. taltalensis grows to a height of only 4 inches (10 cm) and bears yellow flowers. *C. tenuissima* has thin spines and also bears yellow flowers.

Corryocactus

Origin This species ranges from Peru to Chile. It was described by two important cactus authorities: N. Lord Britton (1859–1934) and J. N. Rose (1862–1928). Species formerly included in the separate genus *Erdisia* are now also listed under *Corryocactus*.

Habit These gray-green cacti grow like shrubs, though some are also low-growing to running. Typical of *Corryocactus* species is their very strong and long spination. Spines of up to 10 inches (25 cm) are found in some species. The flowers are yellow to orange or red.

Care *Corryocactus* needs a light, slightly acidic soil. Lime fertilizers must be avoided. If it has a cool spot in winter and practically no water, it blooms profusely. In summer, it can stay outdoors. All varieties are frost-hardy.

Propagation Propagation is from seed and by cuttings. Grafting is recommended.

Species *C. ayopayanus* grows up to about 5 feet (150 cm) high and branches in maturity. The flowers are a strong reddish orange and develop from gray areoles.

The flowers of *C. brachypetalus* are orange and the fruits are edible.

C. brevistylus has yellow blossoms.

The rare *C. matucanensis* bears yellow blossoms and is low-growing to erect.

The flowers of *C. melanotrichus* are red.

C. spiniflorus and *C. squarrosus* have yellowish-red flowers.

Corryocactus matucanensis

Corryocactus ayopayanus

INFO

This genus is a memorial to the chief engineer of the Peruvian railroad, T. A. Corry, who was a supporter of cactus exploration in the Andes.

TIP

Frequent spraying of *Coryphantha* prevents spider mite infestation.

Coryphantha odorata

Coryphantha elephantidens

Coryphantha elephantidens

Origin *Coryphantha* is found from the south of the United States to southern Mexico. This species was described by the French cactus authority A. C. Lemaire (1800–1871). Some species formerly were listed under the genera *Cumarinia* and *Lepidocoryphantha.*

Habit This warty cactus with beautiful spination is globular or in some cases columnar. The flowers, usually yellow, grow directly out of the crown. There are also species whose blossoms are red or white. *C. elephantidens* is compact, globular and only 8 inches (20 cm) thick. The warts are thick and long, the flowers a beautiful deep pink. The spines have a yellow tone.

Care *Coryphantha* is very sensitive to moisture and has a dormant period in midsummer as well as in winter. In these two phases it should be placed in a very light location and kept relatively dry. The root neck should not come into contact with water. Regular cactus soil is used as potting mix.

Propagation Propagation is from seed.

Other Species *C. clavata* bears yellow flowers.

C. cornifera is beautifully spined and bears lemon-yellow flowers.

C. odorata formerly was listed under the genus *Neolloydia* and has whitish-yellow flowers. Dead plants have an odor of sweet woodruff.

The flowers of *C. poselgeriana* are initially yellow, later pink.

C. radicans has lemon-yellow flowers.

Denmoza erythrocephala

Origin The species *Denmoza* comes from the north of Argentina. It was described by the two cactus authorities N. Lord Britton (1859–1934) and J. N. Rose (1862–1928).

Habit At first *D. erythrocephala* is globular, later growing to form a column 5 feet (1.50 m) high. The long, dark, shimmering red spines are surrounded by clusters of bristles and hairs. The red flower, which has violet petals, does not open fully.

Care *Denmoza* needs cactus soil with a little humus as the potting medium. Be sure to avoid full sun in summer. An airy location is important. In winter it should be kept at about 32°F (0°C) and should be given water only sparingly.

Propagation Propagation is from seed.

Other Species The only other species is **D. rhodacantha,** and many cactus authorities mention only this species. However, **D. rhodacantha** gets wider and more globular than **D. erythrocephala.** Its spines and flowers are bright red.

Some older sources also classify the two species under the genera *Echinocactus, Cleistocactus,* and *Pilocereus.*

Denmoza erythrocephala

Denmoza rhodacantha

INFO

The noted cactus specialist Curt Backeberg also found a form with yellow spines in Argentina, which is classified as *D. erythrocephala.*

Discocactus horstii

Discocactus albispinus

Discocactus horstii

Origin This cactus does well in pure quartz sand. It comes from Brazil (Mato Grosso) and was discovered at an altitude of about 3,900 feet (1,200 m). In the current nomenclature most species are classified in other genera, e.g., *Melocactus*. This cactus was established by the cactus scholar and physician L. G. K. Pfeiffer (1805–1877), of Kassel, Germany.

Habit The body of *D. horstii* is a flattened ball that grows only about 2¾ inches (7 cm) wide. The spines have a brown or gray and white bloom. The ribs are prominent. At 2²/₈ inches (6 cm) in diameter, the white, delicately scented flowers seem huge; they bloom only when it is very hot.

Care The planting mix should contain quartz sand and be free of lime. Frequent spraying or misting does *Discocactus* good.

Propagation Propagation is from seed.

Other Species ***D. albispinus*** grows as a flattened ball; its white flowers open at night. ***D. heptacanthus*** has white-pink flowers, while ***D. zehntneri*** bears pure white blossoms.

Disocactus

Origin This cactus lives in tropical Central America—in Honduras and Guatemala—as an epiphyte, that is, a plant that perches on trees and shrubs. *Disocacti* are among the species threatened with extinction. John Lindley (1799–1865), the famed British botanist, described this genus in 1845. Lindley was the secretary of the Royal Horticultural Society in London for 40 years.

Several species formerly were classified under *Phyllocactus* and *Rhipsalis,* as well as under *Bonifazia, Wittia,* and *Wittiocactus.* Today the species *D. nelsonii* belongs to the genus *Chiapasia.*

Habit The main stems of these epiphytic cacti are round, while at the ends they become broad and leaflike and are more or less notched. Spines are completely absent in *Disocactus.* The flowers remain small and resemble a narrow tube that does not appear to open fully.

Care This cactus, which grows in the shade of the trees in its native habitat, should never be exposed to full sun. It needs a humous soil rich in nutrients, but which should contain practically no lime. *Disocactus* is also well suited for hydroponic culture, especially the species *D. eichlamii.* When dormant, it should be kept very dry at about 40°F (4.4°C).

Propagation Like most epiphytic cacti, this genus is also propagated by cuttings.

Species *D. biformis* is bushy and has red flowers whose petals spread. The main stems are roundish; only their ends are broadened like leaves.

D. eichlamii was named after the Thuringian cactus collector, F. Eichlam, who collected cacti particularly in Guatemala. In its native habitat, this species grows in the crowns of trees and hangs down in bushy fashion. The stems are usually about 8 inches (20 cm) long and 2 inches (5 cm) wide. The narrow flowers grow about $2^1/_2$ inches (6–7 cm) long; the few petals are reddish. The stamens project far out.

D. ramulosus has whitish-green flowers and is found in Brazil, Peru, and Bolivia.

TIP
Since in its native habitat *Disocactus* is able to absorb the nighttime dew through its leaves, it should be sprayed after winter dormancy, when the roots are not yet fully functioning, because then it can absorb and distribute the droplets of water.

Disocactus biformis

Disocactus eichlamii

TIP

If the plant body becomes purplish, *Echinocactus* is getting too much sun; then you **must** give it shade!

Echinocactus horizanthalonius

Echinocactus
Hedgehog Cactus

Origin This huge globular cactus (except for the species *E. horizanthalonius,* all species, like *Ferocactus,* are very large) is native to the hot plateaus of Mexico and the deserts of the southwestern United States. The genus was described by the Berlin botanists H. F. Link (1767–1851) and C. F. Otto (1783–1856). Today many of its former species are listed under the following genera: *Aztekium, Denmoza, Echinofossulocactus, Escobaria, Ferocactus, Gymnocalycium, Homalocephala, Matucana, Neolloydia, Neoporteria, Pediocactus, Sclerocactus, Strombocactus,* and *Thelocactus.*

Habit *Echinocactus* has numerous ribs, which are very pronounced. The spines generally are very strong and often are straight or only slightly

Echinocactus grusonii

curved. The flowers remain relatively small.

Care *Echinocactus* needs a sunny and warm spot in its growing season. It is sensitive to moisture; therefore, only newly repotted plants should be watered from the top. All well-rooted hedgehog cacti should be watered from the bottom. *Echinocactus* does well outdoors all summer long, but it must be given protection from rain. The planting mix should contain humus and a little loam. In winter these cacti need to be kept at about 30°F (–1.1°C).

Propagation Propagation is from seed.

Species The best known species is *E. grusonii,* Mother-in-law's Seat. Because of its bright fresh yellow spines, this lush green cactus is also called Golden Barrel Cactus. It only flowers when mature and may become enormous, but it maintains its round shape. When kept indoors, it does not flower at all; it must first have spent some time outdoors. The 2¼-inch (6-cm) long blossoms are yellow inside and brownish outside.

E. horizonthalonius, which is found in desert regions in the southwestern United States as well as in northern Mexico, has horizontally curled spines. This cactus stays relatively small, growing to only 10 inches (25 cm) in diameter. Its body has a gray powdery bloom. The spines run to reddish brown. The small, reddish flowers grow to only slightly more than an inch (3 cm).

E. platyacanthus resembles a ball flattened sideways. In culture it reaches a diameter of about 20 inches (50 cm). The body is bright green, its ribs are steep and narrow, the spines curled and yellow to reddish brown. It bears yellow flowers.

Flowers of
*Echinocactus
platyacanthus*

*Echinocactus
platyacanthus*

Echinocereus
Columnar Hedgehog Cactus

Origin This cactus comes from the western United States and from Mexico. It was described by the German physician and botanist Dr. G. Engelmann (1809–1884). Several species were formerly listed *under Echinocactus, Morangaya,* and *Wilcoxia.*

Habit The Columnar Hedgehog Cactus often forms clusters, is sometimes branched, and is relatively small; in addition, its pulp is "soft-fleshed." Its beautiful, bright, relatively long-lasting flowers are spiny, as are the fruits.

Care Echinocereus cacti like to be kept warm and in a bright and airy location. A sandy soil containing loam, which drains well (mix in a little crushed brick) and is slightly acidic, should be used for potting. Species with few spines should not be kept in full sun. Densely spined species tolerate full sun and need not be watered so much. In winter *Echinocereus* is kept dry, very cool (about 30°F [–1.1°C]), and in bright light. Until April the plant should barely be watered, to allow plenty of buds to form. Don't worry about how shriveled the plants get. A few weeks of warmth and moisture are enough for them to recover their beauty.

Propagation Propagation is from seed and by cuttings, but only starting in late May.

Species *E. fendleri* grows to about 6 inches (15 cm) high and forms dense clusters; the flowers are red.

E. pectinatus (formerly *E. dasyacanthus*) has large yellow flowers, which open completely only in full sun.

Page 64:
Echinocereus scheerii

Echinocereus pectinatus

Echinocereus reichenbachii

Echinocereus stramineus

Echinocereus rigidissimus

E. reichenbachii was discovered by F. Reichenbach, a Dresden engineer. The cactus specialist F. Haage, Jr., gave this species its name in 1893. *E. reichenbachii* is cylindrical. The sharp spines are recurved, and are white or reddish brown. The red flowers are covered with fuzzy hair.

E. rigidissimus formerly was considered to be a variety of *E. pectinatus*, but today it is regarded as a separate species. This so-called Rainbow Cactus has various zones of color and has no central spine. The flowers are more than 2¾ inches (7 cm) long and have a diameter of 4 inches (10 cm).

E. scheerii (formerly *E. salm dyckianus*) grows up to 6 inches (15 cm) high and forms dense clusters. The thorny spines are

Echinocereus subinermis

arranged radially. The gorgeous, long, orange-red funnel-shaped flowers bloom at night; they close up in strong sunlight.

E. stramineus has yellow spines and, even without flowers, stands out in a collection. It grows 8 inches (20 cm) high and, like most cacti of this genus, forms dense clusters. The bright purple flowers are almost the size of the plant itself. The edible fruits are globular.

The shape of **E. subinermis** varies depending on age. When it is young, it is round and flat; in maturity it becomes elongated. Only young plants have spines, while older ones have heavy bristles. The large flowers, almost 4 inches (10 cm) wide, are bright yellow.

Echinocereus fendleri

TIP

The species *E. fendleri* was named after its discoverer: A. Fendler found this cactus in 1849.

Echinofossulocactus
lamellosus

Echinofossulocactus
vaupelianus

Echinofossulocactus

Origin This globular cactus from northern Mexico is very undemanding; thus, is a rewarding plant for "cactus beginners." George Lawrence, the British cactus specialist, described this genus, rich in species, in 1841. Older sources list some species under the genera *Echinocactus* and *Stenocactus*.

Habit These cacti form a ball that, in maturity, can assume the shape of a club. The characteristic feature of *Echinofossulocactus* is its many ribs, which may number up to 100 in old specimens. Plants of the genus, therefore, are called Brain Cacti (*fossula* is Latin for "little furrow"). The upper ribs sometimes shade the lower part of the plant, producing slight discolorations there, which, however, are normal. The number, shape, and color of the spines vary in each species. The small to medium-sized flowers come out of the crown in very early spring.

Care A sandy cactus soil is just right for these species. Fertilize no more than twice in summer. But water generously all summer long. In winter, too, if the plants are kept just a little cooler, water them more often than other cacti. This requirement is related to the large assimilation surface provided by the numerous ribs (lamellae). This cactus may be kept in full sun, but then it should be watered only from the bottom to avoid burn marks.

Propagation Propagation is from seed, in clean moist sand.

Species *E. albatus* has ¾-inch (2-cm) white flowers.

E. coptonogonus has whitish flowers that are crimson in the center.

E. crispatus actually has purple blossoms, but specimens with white flowers and purple median stripes are also found.

E. gladiatus is a still somewhat unfamiliar cactus with peculiar spination. Flower color is reported to be yellow as well as violet.

E. lamellosus has a blue-green body with about 30 very wavy ribs. This species grows to 4 inches (10 cm) high, with a diameter of 2 inches (5 cm). The two-toned reddish flowers are ½ inch (4 cm) long.

E. multicostatus has more than 100 wavy ribs; the flower is white with a violet center.

The flowers of *E. phyllacanthus* are yellowish white with a reddish center.

E. vaupelianus delights the eye with dense whitish spines that project radially on all sides.

E. violaciflorus bears violet flowers, although it also produces whitish ones.

Echinofossulocactus multicostatus

Echinofossulocactus albatus

TIP

Although this cactus also grows on its own roots, it flowers much sooner when it is grafted.

Echinopsis
Sea Urchin Cactus

Origin Munich botanist J. G. Zuccarini (1797–1848) established the genus *Echinopsis,* which is widespread in South America. Hardly any other genus of cactus has undergone so many changes in the classification of its species as this one. Some species have been listed under *Cereus, Chamaecereus, Lobivia, Pseudolobivia, Setiechinopsis, Soehrensia,* and *Trichocereus.*

Habit The spination of *Echinopsis* is quite plain. But it produces beautiful flowers that seem huge in comparison with the body of the cactus. The flowers open in the evening and bloom all night long. Some stay open for 36 hours. They send out a delicate scent. They resemble a funnel with a wide opening and shine in colors of white, yellow, pink, red, and violet. Older specimens often lose their roundish shape and grow upward in columnar form.

Care *Echinopsis,* also commonly called Farm Cactus, is one of the easiest-care cacti around. A sandy cactus soil is just right for these species. They may be placed outdoors in summer, but full sun should be avoided.

Echinopsis needs a potting medium rich in nutrients, to which fertilizer should be added throughout the summer. The medium should be slightly acidic. Keep *Echinopsis* cool in winter; 30°F (–1.1°C) is satisfactory. Only then do the plants come into bloom, even

Echinopsis tubiflora

profusely. Practically no water should be given in winter. Actual watering is begun only when the flower bud has already gotten big. Then a flower of great beauty and size will shortly open on a very plain-looking cactus.

Propagation *Echinopsis* can be propagated by cuttings and from seed. In my experience, cuttings bloom more readily.

Species At first ***E. aurea*** is globular, becoming elongated as it matures. This species grows no bigger than 4 inches (10 cm) and produces yellow flowers of the same size.

TIP

After winter dormancy, I water this genus only when the buds are bigger than $1/2$ inch (1 cm). Then they don't get "stuck" but really burst into bloom.

Echinopsis chrysochete

E. mamillosa var. *kermesina*

TIP

E. chamae-cereus is an indicator plant for spider mites, because it reacts very sensitively to even a few mites.

INFO

Echinopsis pasacana is used as lumber for building.

Echinopsis kratochviliana

Echinopsis mirabilis

E. chrysantha also bears yellow flowers, which open wide and vary from deep yellow to orange.

E. chrysochete has red blossoms with a light throat.

E. kratochviliana is flat and round and never grows bigger than 2⅜ inches (6 cm) in diameter. Sometimes its dark green body is tinged with red. The white flowers, 2 inches (5 cm) wide, have black hairs.

As its name indicates, *E. mamillosa* var. *kermesina* has crimson flowers. This *Echinopsis* may reach a size of 6 inches (15 cm). The body is green, the flowers are about 7 inches (18 cm) long and funnel-shaped. The other thing that is nice about them is that they stay open for 3 days and nights.

The flower of *E. mirabilis* is always a great surprise: It is 4½ inches (12 cm) long, white, and opens at night with a pleasant scent. The small, narrow, columnar body grows only 6 inches (15 cm) high, with a diameter of ¾ inch (2 cm). Its spines and brownish-green color make it very dark.

E. spachiana: This columnar cactus, which reaches 6½ feet (2 m), has yellow-brown spines. The stems, however, are only 2⅜ inches (6 cm) in diameter. The white flowers are 7¾ inches (20 cm) long (see photograph on page 1).

E. tubiflora is 4¾ inches (12 cm) and has white flowers that resemble 7¾-inch (20-cm) long trumpets.

E. backebergii makes crimson flowers.

E. pasacana grows to 33 feet (10 m) high, forms side stems 12 inches (30 cm) thick, and has white flowers 7¾ inches (20 cm) long.

Epiphyllum
Orchid cactus

Origin This orchid cactus comes from Central America and is sometimes still known under the former names *Marniera* or *Phyllocactus*. The British gardener and botanist A. H. Haworth (1768–1833) gave *Epiphyllum* its name. Today some species are included in the genera *Chiapasia, Hatiora, Nopalxochia, Rhipsalis,* and *Schlumbergera*.

Habit The stems of *Epiphyllum* are petiolated and resemble fleshy leaves. The flowers, which open at night, are usually cream-colored, white, yellowish, or reddish, and have elongated tubes. The large

Epiphyllum hybrid

Epiphyllum chrysocardium

flowers are borne laterally and the tubes are covered with scales. Some stems grow upright, while some bend and hang down, so they can also be used as attractive hanging plants. In its native habitat, *Epiphyllum* grows as an epiphyte.

Care This genus cannot tolerate full sun. It should be brought outdoors in summer, but placed only in the shade! The potting medium should consist of a little rotted leaf mold and humus or compost mixed in with regular cactus soil. Generous watering is required; in winter, when the plant is dormant, it still needs to be watered, but then more sparingly.

Propagation Propagation is by stem cuttings.

Species *E. anguligerum* is also called Sawblade or Fishbone Cactus. The stems are thin, flattened, and deeply serrated. Sometimes this species forms a few light-colored bristles. *E. anguligerum* is native to Mexico and has yellowish flesh-colored flowers 3 inches (8 cm) in diameter that open at night.

E. chrysocardium also comes from Mexico and has broad-lobed, bright green stems that are notched like a fern all the way to the central rib. This species grows as an epiphyte and has gorgeous flowers that grow up to a foot (32 cm) long. When they are wide open, the projecting stamens provide additional ornamentation (see photograph on page 39). The outer petals are a pink-brown, the inner ones white. This beautiful species was long known as *Marniera chrysocardium.*

E. oxypetalum is at home not only in Mexico but also in Guatemala, Brazil, and Venezuela. It branches extensively, older stems sometimes growing 10 feet (3 m) long and slightly pendant. These stems are slightly notched and are pointed at the ends. The foot-long (30-cm) flowers are fragrant and are white inside and reddish outside.

E. pittieri even forms a trunk. The margins of the stems are deeply notched like stairs. The flowers of this Costa Rican species are relatively small and from white to greenish. Sometimes reddish scales form on the flowers.

E. crenatum has cream-colored to greenish, scented blossoms.

E. hookeri produces 8-inch (20-cm) white flowers.

The white blossoms of *E. stenopetalum* are also scented.

E. strictum bears white flowers.

E. thomasium has very large, white or yellowish-toned blossoms.

While pure species plants are hard to obtain commercially, many *E. hybrids* are available. These are the well known large-flowered *Epiphyllums* that since 1824 have been obtained from crosses of various species of the genera *Helio-cereus, Nopalxochia, Selenicereus, Cereus,* and *Epiphyllum.* The results of these hybrids are splendid bloomers in many colors, several of which are shown on these pages.

Top, bottom, and page 74: Various *Epiphyllum* hybrids

TIP

As soon as the plants have set buds, I feed them once each week with a weak solution of fertilizer.

INFO

According to the cactus scholar C. Backeberg, this genus is a relic, that is, a surviving remnant of a formerly widely distributed strain.

Eriosyce ceratistes: Growth habit (top) and flowers (bottom).

Eriosyce ceratistes

Origin This globular cactus comes from Chile. It can be found in lowlands as well as at elevations of 6,600 feet (2,000 m) above sea level. The German-Chilean botanist and zoologist R. A. Philippi (1808–1904) described the genus *Eriosyce*.

Habit Globular *Eriosyce* grows up to 20 inches (50 cm) high. Its crown is woolly. The black spines are strong, some growing more than an inch (3 cm) long; the central spine is curved. The flowers are red and may be up to ½ inch (3 to 4 cm) across. *Eriosyce* has a maximum of about 20 ribs, but the number increases with the increasing age of the plant.

Care This genus prefers a rich sandy cactus soil as the planting mix. In the summer it likes bright light and even some sun. Lots of fresh air is good for it. It should be watered generously during the summer. In winter this plant should not be kept below 32°F (0°C) and should then be watered only occasionally.

Propagation Propagation is from seed and by grafting of cuttings; grafted plants are more vigorous.

Other Species The current nomenclature indicates only this one species, to which additional, previously recognized species, such as **E. lapampaensis** and **aurata,** today belong. Some botanists now consider the name *E. ceratistes* to be invalid and classify the species as **E. sandillon.** Several species formerly were listed under the following genera: *Chileorebutia, Delaetia, Horridocactus, Neochilenia, Neoporteria, Pyrrhocactus, Rodentiophila,* and *Thelocephala.*

Escobaria tuberculosa

Origin This warty cactus is found in the United States and in Mexico. The genus was described by the two botanists N. Lord Britton (1859–1934) and J. N. Rose (1862–1928). Older sources listed these species under the following genera: *Cochiseia, Coryphantha, Echinocactus, Gymnocactus, Neobesseya,* and *Mammillaria.*

Habit The gray-green plant grows up to 7 inches (18 cm) high; its freely offsetting stems are almost 2½ inches (6 cm) thick. The white spines have dark tips. Small pink flowers emerge from the crown.

Care *Escobaria* likes a potting medium of sandy cactus soil. Good drainage is important. It cannot be hot and sunny enough for *Escobaria* in summer. In winter, on the other hand, this plant needs a very cool (at most about 30°F [–1.1°C]) and dry location.

Propagation Propagation is from seed, but grafted plants are more vigorous.

Other Species *E. dasyacantha* has numerous whitish, bristly spines. Its central spines are shorter than the blackish brown radial spines. The flowers grow about ½ inch (1.5 cm) across, are a creamy pink, and have a brown median stripe. This species was formerly included in the genus *Mammillaria.*

    E. chihuahensis bears purple blossoms.

    E. emskoetteriana has white flowers with a green center.

    E. missouriensis has greenish-yellow flowers.

    The blossoms of *E. roseana* are reddish.

    E. vivipara has bright pink blooms.

    The flowers of *E. zilziana* are yellow.

INFO

When completely dry, *Escobaria vivipara* withstands frost and snow.

Escobaria tuberculosa

Escobaria dasyacantha

Espostoa

Origin This shrubby cactus, resembling *Cereus,* comes from Peru. N. Lord Britton (1859–1934) and J. N. Rose (1862–1928), the two cactus authorities, established this genus in 1920. Some species were later reclassified by the Austrian botanist F. Buxbaum (1900–1979). Species formerly were found under *Binghamiana, Cephalocereus, Cereus, Facheiroa, Neobinghamiana, Pseudoespostoa, Trixanthocereus,* and *Vatricania.*

Habit This columnar cactus grows like a tree or shrub to a height of 6–13 feet (2–4 m). It commonly branches at the base or in the upper region, depending upon the species. Its stems are usually densely covered with fine hairs. The stem tips end in a cephalium that is located in a very narrow depression with a whitish, yellowish, or brownish hairy covering.

The spines of *Espostoa* are often short, thin, and yellowish, but they may also be white or reddish. The flowers emerge from the cephalium and open at night.

Care The planting medium should be a loamy, slightly acidic cactus soil. In summer *Espostoa* should be kept in a sunny and open spot. To keep the dense, hairy covering clean, do not water from the top. In midsummer give the plant a short break from watering.

Espostoa is best kept in a bright and very cool (around 30°F [–1.1°C]) spot in winter, when it should also be kept dry.

Espostoa lanata

TIP

The genus was named in honor of the Peruvian botanist N. Esposto.

Espostoa melanostele

Propagation Propagation is from seed, by cuttings, and by grafting.

Species *E. lanata* forms a trunk and grows up to 13 feet (4 m) high. The stems grow erect. The whitish-green flowers are 2 inches (5 cm) across.

   E. melanostele branches from the bottom and grows only 6⅕ feet (2 m) high. The white flowers are 2¼ inches (6 cm) wide.

   E. ruficeps branches in the lower half, has whitish hairs, and bears reddish bristles. It forms red-brown, slender cephalia and has white flowers.

   E. blossfeldiorum has yellowish flowers.

   The flowers of *E. guentheri* are cream-colored.

   E. ritteri has large, white blossoms and exhibits interesting tree-like branching.

Espostoa ruficeps

Ferocactus fordii

Ferocactus latispinus

Ferocactus
Barrel Cactus

Origin *Ferocactus* was described by the botanists N. Lord Britton (1859–1934) and J. N. Rose (1862–1928) in 1922. The genus is found in the southwestern United States and the high limestone altitudes of Mexico. Some species previously were listed under these genera: *Bisnaga, Echinocactus, Hamatocactus,* and *Thelocactus.*

Habit Because of its shape, which resembles a barrel when the plant is mature, this large globular cactus is also called Barrel Cactus. Its spines are very strong and, owing to their bright colors, very showy. Sometimes the central spine is larger and wider.

Care It is very difficult to bring *Ferocactus* into bloom indoors. Nevertheless, no collection is complete without it, because the gorgeous spines are its real ornament. *Ferocactus* needs a potting mix of loamy, slightly acidic cactus soil. In summer it should be kept in a warm and sunny location, preferably a window with southern exposure. It grows very slowly; but it should not be excessively fertilized to induce more rapid growth! In winter it needs a cool (about 30°F [–1.1°C]), bright, dry spot.

Propagation Propagation is from seed.

Species *F. fordii* is globular and grows a little bigger than 4 inches (10 cm) It has light red flowers. The radial spines, needle-thin, are white; the central spines are curved hooklike.

The blue *F. glaucescens* has beautiful yellow spines that are all the same size. Its flowers are also yellow. It prefers acidic soil and needs a great deal of water in summer. At first it is globular, becoming elongated when mature.

The broad-spined *F. latispinus* is known as Devil's Tongue. It is found in Mexico at altitudes of more than 9,800 feet (3,000 m) above sea level and grows to over 1 1/2 feet (50 cm). Its central spines are the most interesting thing about it: They project from whitish to pink radial spines, are flat, point downward, and are curved outward. Their color is an intense red with yellow. The flowers are whitish to pink or purple.

F. wislizeni grows to 6 1/2 feet (2 m) high. It is initially globular and then becomes cylindrical. The radial spines are as fine as bristles; only the red central spines are large, curved, and, in some cases, hooked. The flowers are yellow to red.

The flowers of *F. chrysanthus* are yellow; those of *F. cylindraceus* are yellow-orange.

F. echidne has lemon-yellow blossoms, while those of *F. emoryi* are yellow-red.

The flowers of *F. flavovirens* are yellow; *F. gracilis* has yellow flowers with brown stripes.

F. hamatacanthus puts out deep red flowers, while *F. histrix* has light yellow blossoms.

F. macrodiscus has dark red flowers, and the flowers of *F. penisulae* are also red.

F. pilosus (formerly *F. staine-sii,* see photograph on page 8) bears orange flowers, the blossoms of *F. potsii* and *F. robustus* are yellow.

The flowers of *F. viridescens* are yellowish green.

INFO

The crystallized pulp of the Barrel Cactus used to be eaten. Today, in the name of conservation, this is prohibited.

Ferocactus glaucescens

Ferocactus wislizeni

INFO

Many flowers of *Frailea* are cleistogamous, that is, they set seeds without ever fully opening their flowers. The flowers open only in extreme heat.

Frailea cataphracta

Frailea castanea

Frailea cataphracta

Origin This small genus of cactus, which contains many species, is found in Brazil, Paraguay, and Bolivia. The two botanists N. Lord Britton (1859–1934) and J. N. Rose (1862–1928) gave *Frailea* its name in 1922.

Habit *F. cataphracta* is also called the "armored" *Frailea,* because the small, thin spines, less than a tenth of an inch (0.2 cm) long, lie close to the greenish body and thus act like armor. The entire plant grows no bigger than 1½ inches (4 cm); when mature it forms offshoots. The flowers are almost 1½ inches (4 cm) and have a yellow-greenish color.

Care In summer *Frailea* likes to be in a warm and bright spot but not in full sun. It also needs more water at that time. The potting mixture should always be free of lime and have good drainage. In winter *Frailea* should be kept relatively cool, at about 30°F (–1.1°C), and be watered only enough to keep the fine fibrous roots from drying out.

Propagation Propagation is from seed.

Other Species *F. castanea* bears yellow flowers, and has brownish woolly hairs on the outside.

F. colombiana sends out greenish-yellow flowers.

F. gracillima has yellow-red blossoms.

The flowers of *F. grahliana* and *F. knippeliana* are yellow.

F. pumila has small yellow and *F. pygmaea* bristly yellow blossoms.

Today *F. bruchii* is listed under the genus **Gymnocalycium** (see page 84).

Gymnocalycium

Origin This genus, which also contains many species, is distributed throughout almost all of South America. It was described by Dr. L. G. K. Pfeiffer (1805–1877), German physician and cactus scholar. Many species were previously classified as *Echinocactus,* some as *Brachycalycium.*

Habit A general feature of this genus is its "naked" calyx: it is covered only with scales and has no hairs or bristles, and few spines. *Gymnocalycium* is a genus containing many species with generally flattened globular plants. The spines lie close to the body and sometimes may spread out. In most cases the flowers are large and funnel-shaped. Their colors range from white through cream and greenish white to yellow, pink, and red.

Gymnocalycium andreae

Gymnocalycium anisitsii

Gymnocalycium baldianum

Gymnocalycium quehlianum

Care Even in summer, *Gymnocalycium* does not tolerate waterlogging. It is better, therefore, just to sprinkle these plants gently in the evening. Several species of these cacti will come into bloom when they have been kept warm indoors all winter. But then their globular shape becomes deformed. In every case, it is better to overwinter the plants in cool and dry conditions. Cactus soil rich in humus should be used as the potting mix.

Propagation Propagation is from seed. *Gymnocalycium* also lends itself well to grafting.

Species *G. andreae,* with a dark blue-green plant body, comes from Argentina. It attains a size of only 2 inches (5 cm) and develops many offshoots. The flowers are light yellow.

G. anisitsii is globular at first, later becoming elongated, and reaches a size of 4 inches (10 cm). It bears white flowers and comes from Paraguay.

G. baldianum has flowers that are almost blood-red. In a dry location, this species tolerates winter temperatures of as low as 25°F (–3.9°C) for a short time. It should be overwintered in a colder place than other species.

G. bruchii is an Argentine dwarf cactus that produces many offshoots. It has pink bell-shaped flowers and was formerly listed as a *Frailea.*

G. gibbosum, which also comes from Argentina, grows up to 2 feet (60 cm) high. It does not readily form offshoots and bears white flowers.

G. mihanovichii is native to Paraguay and remains dwarfish (2¼ inches [6 cm]). The flowers are yellowish and funnel- or bell-shaped. Many varieties of this species are known. The brightly colored forms of *G. mihanovichii* var. *friedrichii* 'Rubra' (orange-red) and 'Aurea' (light yellow), which can be found in nurseries as grafts, are famed.

G. quehlianum is red to greenish gray. The ribs have been converted into low warty "chins." The large white flowers have a reddish tinge in their throat.

G. cardeniasum has white to pink flowers, while **G. denudatum** has shiny white blossoms.

G. fleisherianum and **G. mazanense** bear pale pink blossoms.

G. monvillei has large white to pink flowers. Those of **G. multiflorum** are light pink.

G. oenanthemum bears winered and **G. platensis** white flowers. **G. saglionis** and **G. schickendantzii** also have white to reddish flowers.

The blossoms of **G. spegazzinii** are white with a red throat.

TIP

Many species have long taproots, so they should be planted in deep pots.

Gymnocalycium mihanovichii

The colorful heads of *Gymnocalycium mihanovichii* var. *friedrichii* in red, orange, and yellow are obtained only by grafting.

Haageocereus multangularis

Haageocereus

Origin This colorfully spined columnar cactus is from Peru, where it grows at sea level as well as at altitudes of up to 7,800 feet (2,400 m) above sea level. The genus was described in 1934 by the German cactus researcher C. Backeberg (1894–1966). It was formerly also classified as *Cereus, Lasiocereus, Maritimocereus, Peruvocereus, Pygmaeocereus,* and *Yungasocereus.*

Habit *Haageocereus* grows in clusters, sometimes erect, sometimes creeping. Since it seldom comes into bloom indoors, its dense spines provide its ornamentation. In most species these are white, yellow, or pink to reddish brown. The flowers are funnel-shaped, greenish, white, or bright red.

Care Care of this cactus presents no problems. In summer it needs plenty of sun and fresh air. Cactus soil that has been enriched with a little loam and sand is the preferred planting mix. Keep it cool in winter (32°F [0°C]), giving it a minimum of water.

Propagation Propagation is from seed and by cuttings.

Species *H. multangularis* grows up to 5 feet (1.50 m) high and tends to form clumps. The color of the fine bristly spines varies from whitish to reddish yellow or brownish. The large funnel-shaped flowers are reddish. The earlier species *H. albispinus,* with yellow spines and light red flowers, also deserves mention here. The large, white 3-inch (8-cm) flowers of ***H. versicolor*** open wide.

H. decumbens has night-blooming white flowers that are brown on the outside.

H. limensis bears white blossoms.

Harrisia jusbertii

Origin Generally speaking, *Harrisia* species are at home in South America, though the native habitat of *H. jusbertii* is not definitely known. The genus was established by N. Lord Britton (1859–1934), well-known geologist and botanist. The species were previously considered to belong to the genera *Eriocereus* and *Roseocereus*.

Habit *H. jusbertii*, the stems of which are only 2 inches (5 cm) thick, is deep dark green. This species is sprawling and tends not to branch. The white flowers grow 7 inches (18 cm) long, are brownish gray on the outside, and open only at night.

Care This is a sturdy plant that is very tolerant of cultural errors. Moisture does it good, so water generously in summer. Use humous cactus soil for potting. *Harrisia* should be overwintered at about 32°F (0°C), and kept dry and in the light.

Propagation Propagation is from seed and by top cuttings.

Other Species *H. tetracantha* is shrubby to treelike in growth. Its stems are 2 ¼ inches (6 cm) thick and bluish green. The greenish flowers grow over 8 inches (20 cm) long. *H. bonplandii*, *H. gracilis*, *H. martinii*, and *H. tortuosa* all have white flowers.

TIP

Harrisia jusbertii is an ideal rootstock for most grafts; it transmits its strength to the scion.

Harrisia tetracantha

Bottom:
Harrisia jusbertii

Hatiora gaertneri

Hatiora x graeseri

Hatiora
Easter Cactus

Origin The Easter cactus is often lumped together with the Christmas cactus (*Schlumbergera*). Actually, however, they belong to two different genera. The Easter cactus comes from the tropical forests of southern Brazil and is a protected plant. The genus was described by the two botanists N. Lord Britton (1859–1934) and J. N. Rose (1862–1928). There has long been a terrible confusion in nomenclature concerning this cactus. The genus has also been listed as *Epiphyllum, Epiphyllopsis,* as *Hariota, Pseudozygocactus, Rhipsalis,* and as *Rhipsalidopsis.*

Habit Easter and Christmas cacti undoubtedly have a great deal in common in appearance, but they also have clear differences in flower and leaf shape: The leaf segments of *Hatiora* are never serrated but are rounded and, as a rule, light reddish.

Hatiora grows epiphytically, forming small bushes with uniformly jointed, flat to angular shoots, which in maturity become round and barklike. The wide-open flowers appear in large numbers at the end of the shoots.

The blooming period, which lasts for two months, usually begins in April. The color range of the flowers includes all shades of red and even yellow.

Care Easter cacti need a little more humidity and warmth than Christmas cacti. And in selecting the potting medium, be sure that it is completely free of lime.

Hatiora can stay indoors all year long, but strong sun should be avoided. Starting in January, put the plant in a cooler place and give it less water. As soon as the first buds begin to appear, it should be moved to a warmer place again and watered more generously. Sprinkle frequently in summer to keep aphids and red spiders away!

Propagation Propagation is by cuttings.

Species *H. gaertneri* has scarlet red flowers and is probably the best known Easter cactus.

H. x graeseri has shiny crimson blossoms. In addition, it is an unusually free-flowering and vigorous plant.

H. rosea, from the southeast of Brazil, is less well-known. It is smaller and bushier and also has smaller flowers. These are a bright light pink and are produced in large numbers.

H. salicorniodes has yellow, bell-shaped blossoms and resembles *Rhipsalis* more than *Hatiora.*

TIP

In order to obtain the necessary acidic medium for Easter cacti, I always mix a little peat in with the cactus soil. Well-rotted leaf mold may be used instead of peat.

Hatiora salicorniodes (top and bottom)

Lepismium
houlletianum

Flowers and fruits of
Lepismium
cruciforme

Lepismium
needs plenty
of light in
winter,
because it
must be kept
warm and
moist.

Lepismium houlletianum

Origin This shrublike cactus comes from Brazil. The genus *Lepismium* was established by the German cactus authority Dr. L. G. K. Pfeiffer (1805–1877). All species formerly were listed under the genus *Rhipsalis;* the nomenclature is still in dispute in some cases. These species have also been attributed to other genera, such as *Acanthorhipsalis, Lymanbensonia,* or *Pfeiffera.*

Habit *Lepismium houlletianum* grows up to 6½ feet (2 m) high. The leaflike stems grow overhanging. They may become 2 inches (5 cm) wide, and are round to cylindrical and deep green. The margins have indentations, in which the whitish, bell-shaped flowers are produced. The stems may also be flat and angular.

Care In summer *Lepismium* should be kept moist and relatively warm. Avoid strong sun. The soil must be rich in humus and slightly acidic. In winter the plant needs a temperature of more than 50°F (10°C) and it should also be kept moderately moist during this time.

Propagation Propagation is from seed and by cuttings.

Other Species *L. cruciforme* has bell-like white flowers that are reddish on the outside.

L. ianthothele has white flowers with pink sepals.

L. trigonum puts out wheel-shaped, whitish to reddish blossoms.

Leuchtenbergia principis

Origin This interesting, small blue-green cactus comes from Texas and northern Mexico. It was described in 1848 by the British botanist Sir W. J. Hooker (1785–1865).

Habit The striking thing about this cactus is its triangular tubercles, about 4 inches (10 cm) long, which project at an angle from the center. At their tips are light, slightly curved bristles. Older specimens of *L. principis* form offshoots and clusters. The large yellow flower, whose tube has reddish scales, emerges at the top from the center of the plant.

Care *Leuchtenbergia* needs a potting medium of sandy cactus soil. In summer it likes to be kept warm and in a sunny spot. In winter a temperature of 32°F (0°C) is satisfactory; it must then be kept dry.

Propagation Propagation is from seed; however, the hard seeds must first be soaked in warm water for several hours. Propagation by grafting is also possible.

Other Species This species, *L. principis,* is the only known representative of the genus ***Leuchtenbergia.***

INFO

This species is found in Mexico, in the Sierra de la Paila, at an altitude of 6,000 feet (1,800 m) above sea level.

Leuchtenbergia principis

INFO

Among Native Americans, *Lophophora,* as peyote, is considered to be sacred and is used in religious ceremonials. Because of its high alkaloid content, the plant may not be collected in or introduced into the United States.

Lophophora williamsii
Peyote, Mescal Button

Origin The Irish physician Dr. T. Coulter (1793–1843) created the genus *Lophophora.* This cactus grows in Texas and northern Mexico and is called Mescal Button because it contains the narcotic mescalin in its plant body. Indoors, however, mescalin is not produced. This genus was formerly called *Anhalonium,* and a variety (var. *lutea*) was classified as *Echinocactus.*

Habit *L. williamsii* has soft pulp and is spineless. The greenish to bluish plant body has felty tufts. The small pink flowers emerge from the crown.

Care This cactus grows well as a graft. *L. williamsii* is sensitive to standing water at the root neck. The cactus soil, therefore, should contain plenty of sand. In summer the plant should have a sunny location. In winter it must be kept dry and cool at 30°F (−1.1°C).

Propagation Propagation is from seed and by grafting.

Other Species The only known species is *L. williamsii;* no other forms are considered species.

Lophophora williamsii

INFO

The name *Mammillaria* is derived from *mamma*, Latin for nipple.

Mammillaria aureilanata

Mammillaria
Pincushion Cactus

Origin *Mammillarias* are found in the United States as well as in Central America. Most pincushion cacti, however, are found in Mexico. This genus was described by the British gardener and botanist A. J. Haworth (1768–1833). Some of the over 150 species of *Mammillaria* were formerly listed under the following genera: *Bartschella, Chilita, Cochemiea, Dolichothele, Ebnerella, Escobaria, Krainzia, Leptocladodia, Mamillopsis, Mammilloydia, Neolloydia, Neomammillaria, Oehmea, Phellosperma, Porfiria, Pseudomammillaria,* and *Solisia.*

Mammillaria bocasana

*Mammillaria
brauneana*

*Mammillaria
camptotricha*

*Mammillaria
densispina*

Habit In this genus, the ribs have been modified to nipples or tubercles. *Mammillarias* are globular to cylindrical. Most of them form clusters, and offshoots can be used for propagation. This genus is among the freely blooming cacti that put on a magnificent display of flowers even with very little care. The small starlike blossoms form a ring around the top of the plant. Since they all open at almost the same time, they make a beautiful show. Some species form several such rings right away. After the flowers fade, the red or yellowish and orange fruits are also attractive. Most *mammillarias* have a thick coat of variably colored spines.

Care *Mammillarias* grow quite fast, although they do not get huge. They are undemanding in terms of care, but one rule of thumb should be noted: Heavily spined, white forms may be kept in full sun. Green specimens with few spines have no protection against the light and should be placed in a location that is bright but does not get full sun.

Propagation Propagation is from seed, by cuttings, or by grafting.

Species *M. aureilanata* comes from Mexico and grows about 3 inches (8 cm) high. Its fine radial spines produce a dense, white-yellow covering of hair. It sometimes lacks central spines. The flowers range from white to light pink.

M. bocasana is easy to care for. Its fine, grayish-white coating of bristles is an added adornment to the brownish central spines, the lower one of which is slightly hooked. The flowers are yellowish with a red-brown center. *M. bocasana* is one of those species that flowers readily year after year. The plant grows no bigger than 2 inches (5 cm).

M. brauneana is globular at first and later elongates to form a club. Yet this cactus has a diameter of only about 3 inches (8 cm). The gray-green tubercles are broad; white bristles emerge from the white woolly axils. The radial spines are dense and also white. The red-

Mammillaria gracilis

Mammillaria guelzowiana

Mammillaria hahniana

Mammillaria herrerae

Mammillaria klissingiana

dish central spines are only a tiny bit longer. Its bright red-violet flowers are the most distinctive feature of the plant.

M. camptotricha is very green and grows in clumps. The radial spines are intriguingly twisted and are white-yellow. The small white flowers have a green stripe in the center. They are quite inconspicuous, but their delicate scent compensates for their plain appearance.

M. candida grows 5½ inches (14 cm) in diameter and is completely covered with dense, white bristles and snow-white spines. The ½-inch (1.5-cm) flowers are pink and have a white margin.

M. densispina is an interesting species: Initially it is globular; later it becomes elongated. The plant body is light at the bottom and becomes yellow to red toward the top. The spines are fine and are produced in abundance. In maturity they get darker, the whitish yellow becoming almost a brown. The light yellow blossoms are ¾ inch (2 cm) across.

M. elongata is small and cylindrical. The round pups develop at the base. The yellow radial spines are less than ½ inch (1 cm) long. The flowers are white to yellowish.

M. gracilis grows about 4 inches (10 cm) high and is cylindrical. The abundant offshoots appear in the upper region of the plant. The numerous radial spines resemble bristles and are white. The longer central spines are brown. The flowers have a whitish-yellow hue.

M. guelzowiana is small and round. The hairy white radial spines are numerous and resemble bristles. The central spines are produced singly but are striking for their hooked shape and reddish to yellowish-brown color. The 2-inch (5-cm) flowers are a bright red.

M. hahniana gets more broad than high (4 inches [10 cm]), forms clusters, and is light green. Its many white radial spines look like tangled hairs. The few white central spines have red tips. The ¾-inch (2-cm) bright purple flowers are also nice.

M. herrerae is a tiny ball, only about 1¼ inches (3.5 cm) in diameter. It seldom forms offshoots. The many white radial spines lie close to the body of the plant. The flowers are a little more than an inch (3 cm) in size and are pale pink to light violet.

M. klissingiana is globular at first and later becomes elongated. The tubercles are produced as an inverted pyramid. The white bristles are very showy and the radial spines are also white. They form an attractive contrast to the ½-inch (1-cm) crimson-red flowers with light green throats.

M. longiflora is a small (about 2 inches [5 cm]), globular species that sometimes also forms pups. The radial spines are white and delicate. The central spines, yellowish to brownish, are somewhat stouter. The striking feature, however, is a fairly long central spine, curved hooklike. The pink flowers are 1½ inches (4 cm) across.

M. microhelia grows as a cylinder of up to 6 inches (15 cm). Offshoots form at the base. The areoles are yellowish. The numerous radial spines, which are yellow and have white tips, are also attractive.

Mammillaria longiflora

Mammillaria microhelia

Mammillaria mystax

*Mammillaria
prolifera*

*Mammillaria
senilis*

With age, brown-red, curved central spines are produced in the upper part of the plant. The flowers are white to greenish, sometimes also with a tinge of pink.

M. mystax is dark gray-green, at first a ball, which grows up to 6 inches (15 cm) high. The axils are woolly white and have wavy bristles. The spines vary in shape and color: The radial spines are white and have brown tips, whereas the central spines are dark red and later become gray. The pink flowers are $^3/_4$ inch (2 cm) in size.

M. nunezii is elongated and grows 6 inches (15 cm) high. Its green plant body is covered by many glassy white spines. The central

Mammillaria schiedeana

spines are a little larger and sometimes the lower one is curved hook-like. The flowers are red. This species formerly was also known as *M. bella*.

M. pottsii (formerly *M. leona*) grows 6 inches (15 cm) high and is dark green. Offshoots develop at the base. The radial spines are a bright white, the central spines heavier and light in color. The flowers stay small, but are a beautiful shade of red.

M. prolifera is small, sometimes no bigger than ¾ inch (2 cm). It forms offshoots freely, so that it always looks like a bunch of balls. The numerous radial spines are white, the central spines yellow. The flowers are yellow with a brown median stripe.

M. schiedeana grows to only 1½ inches (4 cm) but forms dense clusters. The light radial spines are short and sometimes interlaced. There are no central spines at all. This species is one of those that already open their white to yellow flowers in winter.

Mammillaria supertexta

Mammillaria viereckii

Mammillaria zeilmanniana

M. seideliana is globular as well as elongated. The bristlelike radial spines are white and fine. The central spines, also white, are curved hooklike. The flowers are white to light yellow.

M. senilis has dense white radial spines and striking brown, hooklike central spines. The flowers, 2¾ inches (7 cm) long, range from orange to violet. This globular cactus has a diameter of only 1½ inches (6 cm), becoming more elongated as it matures.

M. supertexta is about 2¾ inches (7 cm) and round. Its crown is covered by white radial spines. The central spines are erect and darker. The flowers are light red.

M. viereckii remains small; this round to elongated species grows just 1½ inch (4 cm) broad. The dark green cactus forms many offshoots. The woolly white axils produce bristles. The white radial spines are very small and fine-haired. The central spines, which likewise remain small, are yellow. This species bears whitish flowers with a green midline.

M. wildii can grow up to 6 inches (15 cm) tall. Round pups form at its base. The bristlelike short, radial spines are white and fine. The central spines likewise remain small, but are yellow. The lowest one is hooked. The white flowers are slightly over ¼ inch (1 cm) in diameter.

M. zeilmanniana is globular and later becomes somewhat elongated, but it remains small. The body of the plant is dark green. The fine, white radial spines stand out well against it. The red-brown central spines are short; the lower ones are striking for their hooked shape. This species has very pretty violet flowers.

Matucana

Origin This genus, which was described by the two botanists N. Lord Britton (1859–1934) and J. N. Rose (1862–1928) in 1922, comes from Peru. Older sources also classified species of this genus under *Arequipa, Borzicactus, Echinocactus,* and *Submatucana.* Today the species *M. icosagona* is listed under the genus *Cleistocactus.*

Species grow in various areas of Peru. Thus, *M. aurantiaca, M. haynei,* and *M. weberbaueri,* which are also characterized by fairly dense spination, are found at altitudes of 6,550 to 11,500 feet (2,000 to 3,500 m).

M. ritteri comes from lower altitudes, where it is warmer and, above all, wetter. Its spination, therefore, is not as heavy as that of other species.

Habit As a young plant, *Matucana* is globular; in maturity it develops to form a cylinder. It is usually very heavily covered with spines or with hairs. The ribs are warty and the radial spines are often interlaced with one another. The flowers appear near the crown and are orange to bright red.

Care In the principal growing season, *Matucana* can be kept out in the open in a sunny spot.

It is somewhat sensitive to moisture, however, so it is better to water it too little rather than too much; when repotting, ensure that it has good drainage. This cactus needs a weakly acidic, sandy soil containing loam.

In winter *Matucana* should be kept at 32°F (0°C) and get very little water.

Matucana ritteri

Matucana weberbaueri

INFO

Matucana—like *Schlumbergera*—has zygomorphic flowers; in other words, it has only one plane of symmetry, on which it can be divided into two mirror-image halves.

Matucana aurantiaca

Propagation Propagation is from seed and, for the sake of free flowering, by grafting, since grafted plants bloom considerably faster and more readily.

Species *M. aurantiaca* grows 6 inches (15 cm) high and has dark red and orange flowers. The flowers grow 3½ inches (9 cm) long. It is solitary, but sometimes also forms offshoots. This species should not be kept too cold in winter, when it also needs a little more moisture than is otherwise customary.

M. haynei is globular to cylindrical. The spines are dark brown to black, the flowers scarlet red to crimson.

M. ritteri is a broad globular cactus that readily forms offshoots; the vermillion flowers have violet filaments.

M. weberbaueri (formerly *M. myriacantha*) grows only 2½ inches (7 cm) high but 6 inches (15 cm) wide, which makes it look round and squat. Initially the spines are reddish brown, later almost black. The flowers are a lemon-yellow, though sometimes also pink or orange-red.

Melocactus
Melon Cactus

Origin This cactus comes from Mexico, Brazil, and South America. It was described by two German cactus experts, H. E. Link (1767–1851) and C. F. Otto (1783–1856). Linnaeus was also familiar with this genus, calling it *Cactus.*

Habit *Melocactus* does not bloom until it is about 10 years old, when it finishes its vegetative growth and forms a woolly cephalium, shot through with bristles, on the top. The small red flowers unfold there, usually in the late afternoon. Melon Cactus grows as a wide ball at first, elongating as it matures.

Care *Melocactus* needs heat and abundant moisture. The soil should be rich in humus. However, the Melon Cactus will also grow in pure quartz gravel, as discoveries in Brazil (Bahia) attest. It may be kept in the sun. Its principal growing season is in the fall. In winter it needs a temperature of about 35°F (1.7°C); the soil should never be allowed to dry out completely. Once the plants have formed their white and red top—their cephalium—they should not be repotted.

Propagation Propagation is from seed and by grafting of cuttings.

Species *M. caesius* is a blue-green cactus that remains globular and has 10 broad round ribs. At the very top the cephalium, shot through with reddish brown bristles, is striking. The flowers, which open at night, are small and red.

M. glaucescens is a bluish melon cactus that grows to about 5½ inches (14 cm) across. The whitish cephalium is about 2¾ inches (7 cm) across. The small red flowers emerging from it are very attractive.

M. azureus bears dark red flowers and has a blue plant body.

M. curvispinus has small, light red flowers.

M. intortus produces relatively large, pink blossoms.

M. oreas forms tubular, violet flowers.

The flowers of *M. peruvianus* are dark pink.

Melocactus caesius

Melocactus glaucescens

INFO

Once the cephalium develops, the rest of the plant body stops growing.

This genus was named in honor of M. de Monville. Around 1880, in northern France, he had what was then the most famous cactus collection, containing 400 species.

Monvillea spegazzinii

Origin This *Monvillea* species is at home in Argentina. Other species have been found in Brazil and Paraguay. The two botanists N. Lord Britton (1859–1934) and J. N. Rose (1862–1928) described the genus in 1920. Today one species is listed under the genus *Praecereus*.

Habit This columnar cactus remains very slender and grows shrub-like, prostrate, or, with support, climbing. The ribs are flat, the spines fine and not very numerous. Its stems are bluish green and overhanging. A few spines are produced only on young stems. The flowers are a whitish green and open at night.

Care This species likes to spend the summer in a warm and sunny location, at which time it should also be watered generously. In winter *Monvillea* enjoys a temperature of 35°F (1.7°C); water sparingly during this time, but do not let the plant dry out! This cactus likes humous soil.

Propagation Propagation is from seed and by cuttings.

Other Species *M. anisitsii* bears whitish flowers and *M. cavendishii* has large white blossoms.

M. diffusa forms greatly curved white flowers.

The scaly flowers of *M. haageana* are greenish white.

M. lindenzweigiana has whitish blossoms but mottled stems.

The white-flowering *M. pharnosperma* has beautiful spines.

Monvillea spegazzinii

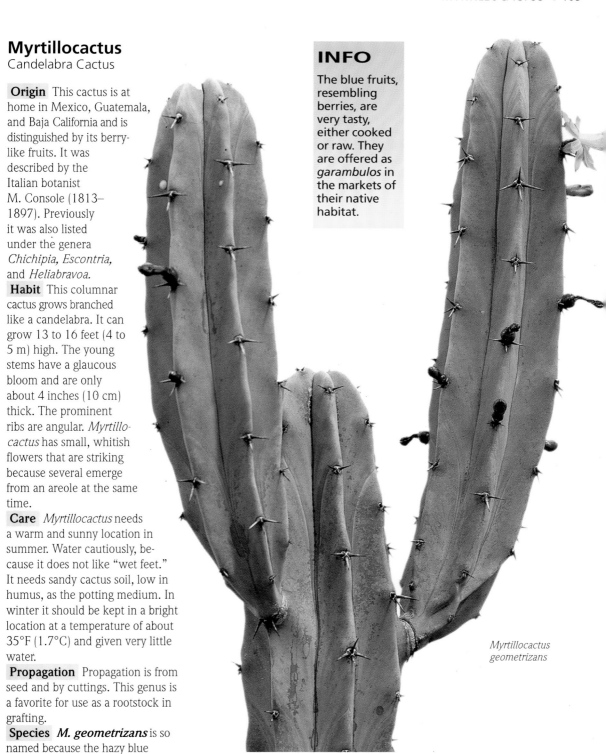

Myrtillocactus
Candelabra Cactus

Origin This cactus is at home in Mexico, Guatemala, and Baja California and is distinguished by its berry-like fruits. It was described by the Italian botanist M. Console (1813–1897). Previously it was also listed under the genera *Chichipia, Escontria,* and *Heliabravoa.*

Habit This columnar cactus grows branched like a candelabra. It can grow 13 to 16 feet (4 to 5 m) high. The young stems have a glaucous bloom and are only about 4 inches (10 cm) thick. The prominent ribs are angular. *Myrtillocactus* has small, whitish flowers that are striking because several emerge from an areole at the same time.

Care *Myrtillocactus* needs a warm and sunny location in summer. Water cautiously, because it does not like "wet feet." It needs sandy cactus soil, low in humus, as the potting medium. In winter it should be kept in a bright location at a temperature of about 35°F (1.7°C) and given very little water.

Propagation Propagation is from seed and by cuttings. This genus is a favorite for use as a rootstock in grafting.

Species *M. geometrizans* is so named because the hazy blue

INFO
The blue fruits, resembling berries, are very tasty, either cooked or raw. They are offered as *garambulos* in the markets of their native habitat.

Myrtillocactus geometrizans

Myrtillocactus schenkii

Neolloydia conoidea

patches on the young stems stand out in geometric lines. Its side shoots grow erect. Initially the radial spines are reddish, while the single central spine is black and shaped like a dagger. The flowers, only a little over an inch (3 cm) across, are whitish green.

M. schenkii is dark green and can grow up to 16 feet (5 m) high. The trunk is actually short, because branching begins quite low down. The stems are very close together and have a diameter of 4 inches (10 cm). This species rarely has a glaucous bloom. The ribs are sharp-edged. The radial spines are barely ½ inch (1 cm) long and sometimes are slightly curved. The single dark central spine sticks straight out and is 2 inches (5 cm) long. The small flowers are whitish to cream-colored.

M. cochal is a magnificently branched cactus with whitish blossoms.

Neolloydia

Origin This genus is native to the United States, Mexico, and Cuba. It consists in large part of species that formerly belonged to other botanical genera, for example, *Coryphantha, Echinocactus, Gymnocactus, Mammillaria, Normanbokea, Pelecyphora, Rapicactus, Strombocactus, Thelocactus, Toumeya,* and *Turbinicarpus. Neolloydia* was described by the two cactus authorities N. Lord Britton (1859–1934) and J. N. Rose (1862–1928).

Habit *Neolloydia* is a little like *Mammillaria*, although it does not have the pretty ring of flowers. But its light gray and brownish-green plant bodies have just as

*Neolloydia
mandragora*

many tubercles. The radial spines generally lie close to the body or are curved and spreading. The central spines often have dark tips and stick out. The cactus may stay small (1 inch [2.5 cm]), but may also grow to 4 inches (10 cm).

Care This genus needs a warm and sunny place in summer. Sandy cactus soil is used as potting mix. *Neolloydia* does not like "wet feet." It should be kept very cool in winter, 32°F (0°C) being satisfactory.

Propagation Propagation is from seed and by grafting.

Species *N. conoidea* resembles a 4 inch- (10 cm-) high barrel with

*Neolloydia
gielsdorfiana*

Neolloydia horripila

Neolloydia pseudomacrochele

woolly axils and whitish-gray spines. The central spines are black. The flowers are about $2\frac{1}{2}$ inches (6 cm) across and reddish violet.

N. gielsdorfiana grows in northeastern Mexico. This globular species, which does not offshoot readily, has a yellow to blue-green plant body. The tubercles are arranged in spirals. The dark brown radial spines grow $\frac{3}{4}$ inch (2 cm) long and are slightly curved. The flowers are white.

N. horripila is roundish, bluish green, and grows to just 4 inches (10 cm). The spines are yellowish to dark brown. The gorgeous flowers can grow to be $1\frac{1}{2}$ inches (4 cm) across and are bright wine-red with a lighter margin.

N. mandragora remains globular and grows to only $2\frac{1}{4}$ inches (6 cm). The thick tubercles are square-shaped. The radial spines are white, as are the central spines, which, also have a brown tip. The 1-inch (2.5-cm) flowers are white with pink stripes.

N. pseudomacrochele stays small and globular. The whole cactus grows no bigger than $1\frac{1}{4}$ inches (3 cm). The elastic spines of various lengths, some of which stick straight out and some of which are interlaced with one another, are striking. They are initially yellowish, later gray. The white flower, $1\frac{1}{2}$ inches (3.5 cm) across, has a light pink median stripe.

N. schmiedickeana at first is globular and small. Later it becomes cylindrical and grows to 2 inches (5 cm). The spines are an inch (2.5 cm) long and bent to curved. Their upper sides are flat. The pink flowers have a violet median stripe.

N. valdeziana stays tiny (only 1 inch [2.5 cm]) and has blue-green tubercles. The fine spines, not even ⅛ inch (2 mm) long, are feathery and lie right on the body of the plant. This species, which comes from Mexico, has violet flowers ¾ inch (2 cm) in diameter. This cactus was formerly listed under the genus *Pelecyphora*.

N. lophophoroides bears white flowers with a delicate pink tinge.

N. pseudopectinata (formerly *Pelecyphora pseudopectinata*) has pale pink flowers with a brown median stripe.

N. saueri has white blossoms.

N. smithii has red flowers.

The flowers of **N. viereckii** are lilac pink.

TIP

I have observed that *Neolloydia conoidea* does considerably better in soil that contains plenty of humus than in regular cactus soil that is poor in nutrients.

Neolloydia schmiedickeana

Neolloydia valdeziana

Neoporteria chilensis

Neoporteria

Origin Chile and Argentina are home to this genus, whose many species previously were often listed under other genera, including *Chilenia, Chileniopsis, Echinocactus, Horridocactus, Islaya, Neochilenia,* and *Pyrrhocactus. Neoporteria* was described by the cactus specialists N. Lord Britton (1859–1934) and J. N. Rose (1862–1928) in 1921.

Habit This roundish cactus, which later often becomes elongated, remains relatively small. Its coating of spines is dense and rich in variants, in both shape and color. The petals are pointed. The flowers range in color from shades of red

Neoporteria islayensis

TIP

I don't like to give *Neoporteria* much water, even in summer.

Neoporteria nidus

Neoporteria subgibbosa

all the way to yellow.

Care *Neoporteria* has a short dormant period in summer, when it is kept dry; otherwise, it needs a semi-sunny location. It should be kept dry and cool in winter (40–45° [5–8°C]). *Neoporteria* needs a loamy, slightly acidic cactus soil as the potting medium. Grafted plants grow faster.

Propagation Propagation is from seed and by grafting.

Species *N. chilensis* has pink-red flowers with long white hairy bristles. At first its shape is globular, becoming almost columnar in maturity. The whitish-/yellow spines are shiny; the central spine is black-brown.

N. islayensis gets very big and tilts over when it is old. The yellow spines remain small and point downward. The fragrant blossoms are over an inch (3 cm) in diameter and bright yellow.

Neoporteria
taltalensis

Neoporteria
villosa

N. nidus remains a ball only at first and then grows to form a cylindrical column. The spines are straight and hard, as well as curved and bristly. Their color varies from whitish through yellow all the way to black. The reddish flowers are more than an inch (3 cm) across.

As a young plant, **N. subgibbosa** is a ball; later it becomes very long. The body of the plant is light green. The areoles are woolly white. The spines are yellow, later darkening to reddish brown. The flowers, almost 1¼ inches (4 cm) in diameter, are crimson pink.

N. taltalensis is a 3-inch (8-cm) ball with warty ribs. The brownish-white spines are straight, curved, or even twisted. The pink-purple to reddish-white flowers, slightly over an inch (3 cm) in diameter, have white woolly hairs.

N. villosa is usually globular, only becoming cylindrical later. This gray-green species grows 6 inches (15 cm) high. The spines are produced in great numbers and resemble fine bristles. The strong central spines are curved, actually blackish, but often with light yellow hairy spines underneath. The flowers are whitish pink.

N. aricensis bears light yellow flowers and is very rare.

N. bulbocalyx is globular and does not form offshoots. Its flowers are yellow.

N. curvispina has straw-yellow flowers.

N. horrida bears brownish flowers with a red median stripe.

N. napina has pale yellow blossoms that are covered with long fuzzy hair and dark bristles.

The flowers of **N. odieri** are white to pink.

Nopalxochia phyllanthoides

Origin This gorgeous flowering cactus, which was described for the first time in 1813 by the physician and botanist A. P. Decandolle (1778–1841) as *Cactus phyllanthoides,* comes from Mexico.

Habit *Nopalxochia phyllanthoides* is a typical leafy cactus. Its stems are at first round, later becoming flat and slightly pendant. It grows epiphytically. Aerial roots develop at the tips of the joints. The many large (3½-inch [9-cm]), pink flowers appear from April to June. This genus was cultivated by the Aztecs as *nopalxochit.*

Care Like all leafy cacti, this one needs heat but not full sun. In summer it is best kept in light shade as a hanging plant. Use humous, slightly acidic cactus soil as the planting medium. In winter, when it should also get less water, the plant should not be kept below about 40°F (4.4°C).

Propagation Propagation is from seed and by cuttings.

Other Species *Nopalxochia* hybrids (= *Phyllocactus* hybrids) bear flowers in all shades of red.

Nopalxochia phyllanthoides

INFO

Nopalxochia phyllanthoides was long known incorrectly as *Epiphyllum phyllanthoides* or *Phyllocactus alatus.*

INFO

Two Mexican statesmen were sponsors at the naming ceremony: President Obregón and Minister Deneger.

Obregonia denegrii

Opuntia rufida

Obregonia denegrii

Origin This cactus was discovered in northeastern Mexico. The Czech cactus specialist A.V. Frič (1882–1944) described the genus in 1925. *O. denegrii* formerly was also listed as *Ariocarpus.*

Habit This flattened globular cactus grows up to 4½ inches (12 cm) wide. It is gray-green and has turned-down scales that are very thick and sharp-edged. The few spines on the tips of the tubercles soon fall off. *O. denegrii* has 1-inch (2.5-cm) white or light pink flowers that emerge from the woolly center.

Care In summer this cactus needs heat and sun but also tolerates some shade. Sandy cactus soil should be used as the potting medium. In winter it must stay cool (32°F [0°C]) and dry.

Propagation Propagation is from seed and by grafting of cuttings (on *Pereskiopsis*).

Other Species *O. denegrii* is the only known species.

Opuntia
Prickly Pear

Origin The range of distribution of *Opuntia* is from Canada to southern Argentina. With some 300 species, *Opuntia* is the genus of the family Cactaceae that has the most species, other than *Mammillaria.* Therefore, I can discuss only a few representative ones here. This genus was described back in 1754 by the English gardener and botanist P. Miller (1691–1771). The current nomenclature now also lists representatives of the genera *Austrocylindropuntia, Brasiliopuntia, Consolea, Corynopuntia, Cumulopuntia, Cylindropuntia, Grusonia, Maihueniopsis, Marenopuntia, Micropuntia, Nopalea, Platyopuntia, Puna,* and *Tephrocactus* under the genus *Opuntia.*

Habit *Opuntia* is called the Prickly Pear because of its fruits, which in most cases are edible. The joints or pads are a general, clearly visible feature of *opuntias.* These padlike stem elements usually stand away from the plant body and are flat and more or less spined. *Opuntia* grows like a shrub or may even be treelike. The flowers, in a great variety of colors, appear at the upper margins of the joints; they are quite large and open wide. Some species have leaves that usually soon fall off.

Care Almost no problems are encountered with *opuntias* if they are not allowed to become waterlogged. They like a light but nutrient-rich cactus soil. *Opuntias* tolerate temperatures around 32°F (0°C) in winter. In summer they like a light and warm location. If they are protected from the sun, most species can also be kept outdoors during the summer.

Propagation Propagation is from seed and by cuttings.

Species *O. alexandri* is globular and gray-green. The knobby stems have a diameter of 1⅛ inches (3 cm). The white spines grow up to 1½ inches (4 cm) long and end in a dark tip. Nothing is known about the flowers.

O. clavarioides is relatively small. The body of the plant is

INFO

Typical of all *opuntias* is the presence of clusters of small, fine hairy spines (glochids), which look soft but are barbed. Therefore, always use gloves when repotting, because these spines are hard to remove and may cause serious irritation of the skin.

Top:
Opuntia alexandri

Opuntia clavarioides

Opuntia microdasys

Blooming
Opuntia rufida
(see also photograph
on page 114)

brownish and branched, like an open hand. The white spines are tiny, fairly close to the body, and resemble bristles. The yellow-brownish flowers are about 2³⁄₈ inches (6 cm) wide.

O. microdasys, Bunny Ears, is also called Golden Opuntia, because its thick delicate clusters of glochids are golden yellow. It branches and becomes a shrub 2 feet (60 cm) high. The round to oval stems grow 6 inches (15 cm) long. The yellow flowers, 2 inches (5 cm) in diameter, are also pretty when they are fading, because they do not just wilt but change color to become reddish.

O. microdasys var. **albispina** has impressive white glochids.

O. rufida comes from Mexico and, like *O. microdasys,* has clusters of glochids, only these are bright red-brown. It bears yellow flowers that turn yellow-orange when they fade.

In Peru, its native habitat, **O. subulata** becomes an awkward-looking bush up to 13 feet (4 m) high; it forms a trunk that is 4 inches (10 cm) thick. The stems come out sideways and have dark-bordered warts. The leaves grow to $4^{3}/_{4}$ inches (12 cm) and remain on the cactus for over a year; then they fall off and after a while sprout out again. The yellowish spines are not very numerous but are 3 inches (8 cm) long. The red flowers are more than $2^{1}/_{2}$ inches (7 cm) in diameter.

O. tunicata has stems that detach readily; it is, therefore, a widely distributed plant, even a nuisance, in its native habitats. This species comes from Mexico, but it is also found in Texas, Ecuador, and Chile. It is low-growing and bushy. The stems are short, becoming at most 6 inches (15 cm) long, and are distinctly warty. The spines grow 2 inches (5 cm) long and are reddish, but they

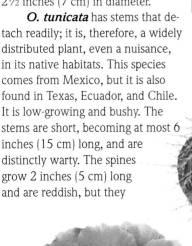

TIP

Opuntia is also a cultivated plant, especially because of its tasty fruit. Mexico, in particular, has large areas of *O. ficus-indica*, the Indian Fig, under cultivation. Cactus fruits were being eaten as long ago as 7000 B.C.E., as discoveries of coproliths (mineralized feces) in Mexican caves reveal. Naturally, the fruits of present-day crops differ from those of the wild form of that time. Meanwhile, virtually spineless forms and varieties with a high percentage of pulp and few seeds have become established.

Top:
Opuntia verschaffeltii

Opuntia erinacea

Opuntia subulata

Opuntia fragilis

bear thin whitish sheaths, which look very decorative. The yellow flowers are more than an inch (3 cm) wide.

O. verschaffeltii is low-growing and has multiple stems. Its limbs are slightly warty and the few spines are soft as bristles. The flowers, orange to deep red, are striking.

There are **winter-hardy opuntias,** which can be left outdoors if they are protected in winter. These include:

O. fragilis, with 2-inch (5-cm) light yellow to reddish yellow flowers.

O. phaeacantha, with red-brown and yellow glochids and yellow flowers almost 2 inches (5 cm) wide.

O. polycantha, which bears 1½-inch (4-cm) light yellow to orange blossoms.

O. erinacea var. **utahensis,** the Porcupine Cactus. It bears rose-pink to orange flowers that grow 3 inches (8 cm) wide.

Oreocereus
Old Man of the Andes

Origin This columnar cactus comes from the high elevations of Argentina, Bolivia, Peru, and Chile, at altitudes of 13,000 feet (4,000 m). The genus *Oreocereus* was established in 1909 by the Italian gardener and cactus researcher V. Riccobono (1861–1943), the director of the Botanical Garden in Palermo. Species formerly listed under the genera *Arequipa, Arequipiopsis, Borzicactus, Cleistocactus, Matucana, Morawetzia, Oroya, Pilocereus,* and *Submatucana* can now be found under *Oreocereus*.

Habit *Oreocereus* grows as a bush or forms low, branched clumps. It is usually heavily covered with hair. The strong spines vary in color. The flowers, scaly on the outside, project slanting near the crown and blossom in the daytime.

Care This cactus needs lots of sun. And it does not mind water. It also likes plenty of fresh air year-round. Cactus soil containing loam and gravel and relatively poor in nutrients should be used as the potting medium, since this makes *Oreocereus* more resistant. In winter it should have a temperature of no lower than 40°F (5°C) and must be kept almost completely dry. When dry, it will tolerate temperatures around 32°F (0°C) for a brief period. But then it should promptly be placed in gradually warmer surroundings.

Flowers are unlikely to form indoors, but because of its heavy coating of hair, *Oreocereus* is one of the most beautiful columnar cacti.

Propagation Propagation is from seed.

Oreocereus celsianus

Oreocereus doelzianus

Oreocereus fossulatus

Oreocereus trollii

Species *O. celsianus* grows over 3 feet (1 m) high, is blue-green, and branches from the base. The stems grow to 4 inches (10 cm) thick. The crown is enveloped in long and dense interlaced strands of hair. The variably colored radial spines grow only $^{3}/_{4}$ inch (2 cm) long. In contrast, the stouter central spines grow to 3 inches (8 cm). The delicate pink flowers are almost 4 inches (10 cm) in diameter.

O. doelzianus is over 3 feet (1 m) high and has 3-inch (8-cm) thick, dark stems that thicken at the end. These all come from the base. The areoles are downy and loosely covered with hair. The radial spines are only $1^{1}/_{8}$ inches (3 cm) long; the 2-inch (5-cm) central spines appear criss-crossed in shades of brown. The cephalium, from which the small red-purple flowers emerge, grows 2 inches (5 cm) long.

O. fossulatus is a loosely branched shrub $6^{1}/_{2}$ feet (2 m) high. Its hairy covering and radial spines are white. The few central spines, $1^{1}/_{2}$ inches (4 cm) long, are yellow to brown. It bears reddish-violet flowers.

O. trollii stays low. Branched at the base, it grows no more than $1^{1}/_{2}$ feet (0.5 m) high. It has thickset stems. It is very attractive with its $2^{3}/_{4}$-inch (7-cm) long, fine and dense hairs, in which the bristlelike radial spines are hard to find. The sturdy central spines, at first red and later brown, provide a beautiful contrast. The flower, $1^{1}/_{2}$ inches (4 cm) wide, is rose-pink to crimson red.

O. hempelianus has red flowers.

O. hendriksenanus bears crimson flowers.

Pachycereus

Origin This cactus is found in the United States and in western Mexico. A. Berger (1871–1931), the Thuringian botanist and cactus scholar, was the first to investigate this cactus, in 1909. However, the description of the genus for the currently accepted nomenclature comes from N. Lord Britton (1859–1934) and J. N. Rose (1862–1928), the two well-known cactus authorities. Occasionally species of *Backenbergia, Cereus, Lemaireocereus, Lophocereus, Marginatocereus, Mitrocereus, Petrocereus, Pilocereus, Ritterocereus,* and *Stenocereus* are also included in this genus.

Habit This cereus is also known as the "Giant Cereus," because although it is generally columnar, it looks more massive than any other *Cereus.* It branches laterally. The stems usually grow upward. Overall, it grows treelike; it forms a thick trunk, which, in comparison to its size as a whole, looks quite low. The cactus can often grow 33 feet (10 m) high, with a trunk only 39 inches (1 m) thick. The trunk tends to become woody in maturity. Ribs are present in large numbers. The spines are strong. The funnel-shaped flowers open at night, sometimes being woolly with bristles and sometimes scaly.

Care This heat-loving cactus requires a place in the sun with plenty of fresh air. It is sensitive to waterlogging. The potting mix, therefore, should be very porous, that is, contain a lot of sand. It is a good idea to have a drainage layer of small pebbles

INFO

Pachycereus pecten-arboriginum is so named because its heavily spined fruit was formerly used as a comb by indigenous peoples.

Pachycereus marginatus

Pachycereus pecten-arboriginum

Pachycereus pringlei

Pachycereus weberi

on the bottom of the pot. Cactus soil requires no additional humus. *Pachycereus* should be kept very cool in winter, 40°F (4°C) being sufficient. It should also be kept quite dry during this period.

Propagation Propagation is from seed.

Species *P. marginatus* is a dark gray-green cactus that forms a trunk 5 feet (0.5 m) high. The stems grow up to 23 feet (7 m) long, with a diameter of 6 inches (15 cm). The areoles are brown and feltlike, and the spines are very short and at first reddish. The white flowers are 2 inches (5 cm) in diameter; they are produced singly or in pairs in an areole.

P. pecten-arboriginum grows more than 33 feet (10 m) high and is thick; its 6½-foot- (2-m-) high trunk has a 12-inch (30-cm) diameter. The stems rise steeply upward. The thick areoles are shieldlike. They appear to be connected by a felt band. The spines on the crown are pale gray, while the spines in the flowering zone are golden brown. The flowers grow 3¼ inches (8.5 cm) long and are pure white.

P. pringlei becomes a thick tree about 36 feet (11 m) high. The stems rise at an angle. Young stems have an arch-shaped powdery bloom. The heavy spines are ¾ inch (2 cm) long; they are white and have black tips. They fall off in the flowering zone. The 3-inch (8-cm) white blossoms have a funnel-like bell shape.

P. schottii grows 10 feet (3 m) high, is yellowish green, and has a powdery bloom.

P. weberi has yellow flowers that are 4 inches (10 cm) in diameter. This species grows 33 feet (10 m) high, the trunk comprising only 3 feet (1 m).

Parodia

Origin These cacti, usually globular, come from Argentina, Bolivia, Paraguay, and Brazil. The genus was named in 1923 by C. Spegazzini (1858–1926), the Italian botanist. He lived in Argentina for many years.

There have been repeated changes in classification of species in this genus, which contains a large number of species. Accordingly, several of them were formerly considered to be in the genera *Acanthocephala, Brasilicactus, Brasiliparodia, Eriocactus, Eriocephala, Malacocarpus, Notocactus,* and *Wigginsia.*

TIP

The genus was named in honor of Dr. D. Parodi, who was the first to explore the flora of Paraguay.

Parodia buiningii

Parodia bueneckeri

Parodia chrysacanthion

Parodia graessneri

Habit The intensely colored spines are straight, curved, or hook-shaped. When the flowering season is over, they provide this little plant with not inconsiderable ornamentation. Yet there are some species that start blooming as early as January. *Parodias* may bloom even as cuttings. Their large flowers, at first funnel-shaped and then opening up wide, are produced in yellow, orange, and red.

Care *Parodia* requires a good cactus soil to promote the formation of fibrous roots. In summer, it likes to be kept in a light location, but not in full sun. It requires plenty of fresh air and abundant water in the principal growing season. Watering should be done from below: otherwise, the plant body develops unsightly marks.

In winter *parodias* like to be kept in a bright and airy spot and at a minimum temperature of 45°F (8°C). They should be kept almost dry, but do not allow the fine fibrous roots to dry out.

In some species, flowering and growth may be promoted by grafting.

Propagation Propagation is from seed and by grafting.

Species *P. bueneckeri* is globular and grows to about 2 inches (5 cm). It is a rich green. The small radial spines are whitish. Some of the brownish central spines are curved; some are produced as hooks. Its bright golden yellow flowers are 1½ inches (4 cm) in diameter.

P. buiningii is cylindrical and

Parodia haselbergii

Parodia herteri

Parodia leninghausii

Parodia mutabilis

can grow 3 inches (8 cm) high. The white areoles are heavily covered with wool. The radial spines are white. The central spines, reddish brown with black tips, stand out. They grow ¾ inch (2 cm) long and remain straight. The yellow flowers are 2 inches (5 cm) across.

P. chrysacanthion is a bright golden-yellow species, its light green, broad globular body being enveloped by numerous fine bristly yellow spines. The central spines are golden yellow as well. The many bright yellow flowers are funnel-shaped.

P. graessneri grows 4 inches (10 cm) high and is broad-globular. Its many ribs have small warts. The yellow spines grow ¾ inch (2 cm) long. The flowers are green and open in late winter.

P. haselbergii grows as round as a ball and 4 inches (10 cm) high. At first the dense spines are yellowish, but later they become white. Numerous fire-red flowers, with their orange margins, emerge from the white coating of spines as early as January.

P. herteri is globular, becoming somewhat cylindrical only in maturity. It has a diameter of 6 inches (15 cm) and is pale green. Its crown is very warty and woolly white. The radial spines are fine as a needle and flexible. At first they grow straight; later they rise radially in different directions. The brown-red central spines are ¾ inch (2 cm) long and intersect one another. The flowers, 1½ inches (4 cm) across, are deep red to purple and have a lighter center. On the outside they are covered with white and brown wool.

P. leninghausii is a very large species that can grow to 3 feet (1 m)

Parodia nivosa

Parodia ottonis

high when mature. At first, however, it is round to broad-globular and has a diameter of 4 inches (10 cm). This species forms many offshoots from the bottom. At the crown, it is provided with numerous woolly bristles. The radial spines also resemble thin yellow bristles. The bristlelike central spines are light yellow and likewise fine. The flowers, 2 inches (5 cm) across, open up flat over the crown. They are yellow; only their sepals are green.

P. mutabilis is globular and grows about 3 inches (8 cm) high. The many fine radial spines are white. The yellowy-brown central spines, which get longer, look stouter. One of them is curved downward in the shape of a hook. The 1½-inch (4-cm) flowers are a deep yellow.

P. nivosa is globular to elongated

Parodia rutilans

Parodia scopa

and may grow up to 6 inches (15 cm) high, with a diameter of 3 inches (8 cm). The plant body is light green; the ribs have been converted into cylindrical warts. The short areoles are covered with white wool. The bristlelike spines are snowy white and fine. The white central spines are a little darker and stouter at the base. The flower, 2 inches (5 cm) in diameter, is fiery red.

P. ottonis remains flat and round and grows about 4 inches (10 cm) high; it is a rich green. The yellow radial spines are fine as needles. The reddish-brown central spines get somewhat heavier. The 2¼-inch (6-cm) flowers are a brilliant deep yellow. Their stigmas are dark red.

P. rutilans is globular and becomes elongated up to 4¾ inches (12 cm) only when mature. Its plant body is a dull blue-green. The areoles are a woolly white. The small radial spines are white at the bottom and brown-red, later becoming yellowish, at the top. The two central spines are bright brown-red. This species bears rose-pink flowers with a lighter throat. The flowers grow up to 2¼ inches (6 cm) in diameter and on the outside are covered with white wool and red-brown bristles.

P. scopa becomes quite large. At first it is globular, but later it may grow to 10 inches (25 cm) high, developing a diameter of 4 inches (10 cm). Its plant body is a lively green. The small, numerous radial spines are white and remain thin. The few central spines are heavier; they are brownish red and also whitish. The 1½-inch (4-cm) flowers are bright yellow and have a red stigma. The tube is covered with brown wool on the outside and bears black bristles.

Pelecyphora
Woodlouse Cactus

Origin This cactus, of which only the two species illustrated are known, comes from northern Mexico. The genus was described in 1843 by Prof. C. G. Ehrenberg (1795–1876), a German medical man and botanist.

P. strobiliformis was formerly considered to be in a genus of its own, *Encephalocarpus.* Today two other species, *P. pseudopectinata* and *P. valdeziana,* are listed under *Neolloydia.*

Habit This small globular cactus forms clusters when mature. The tubercles are compressed sideways and form small warts. The areoles are elongated. The spines lie on the warts like combs. The flowers, red-violet (inside) and greenish white (outside), open only in full sun.

Care *Pelecyphora* likes full sun and lots of heat. For a potting medium, it prefers a little sand in the cactus soil. In winter, this cactus should be kept relatively cool (around 32°F [0°C]) and dry.

Propagation Propagation is from seed and by grafting on *Echinopsis pachanoi* or *Harrisia jusbertii.*

Species *P. aselliformis* is the *Pelecyphora* that has spines resembling a woodlouse. It remains small and round, i.e., it grows no higher than 4 inches (10 cm) at most and then has a diameter of 2 to 2¼ inches (5–6 cm). Its body is gray-green. It is thickened at the base. This species forms offshoots. The tubercles are arranged in spirals. The spines are very small and some stand off like combs on two sides, while some lie on top. Central spines are completely absent. The crimson-violet flowers

TIP

Water *Pele-cyphora* sparingly, even in summer!

Flowers of
*Pelecyphora
strobiliformis*

*Pelecyphora
aselliformis*

INFO

All parts of *Pelecyphora* were formerly used by Native Americans as medicine and a remedy for wounds.

are more than an inch (3 cm) across. They are slightly bell-shaped and emerge from the crown, sometimes several at the same time.

P. strobiliformis remains small and globular. The crown is feltlike, the tubercles are clearly arranged on a slant. The small spines appear only on young plants and soon fall off. The 1-inch (3-cm) flowers that emerge from the crown are bright violet.

Pelecyphora strobiliformis

Pereskia sacharosa

Pereskia

Origin This genus ranges from Florida all the way to South America. P. Miller (1691–1771), British gardener and botanist, established this name in 1754. Sometimes the old spelling *Peireskia* is still used. Some species formerly were listed under the genus *Rhodocactus*.

Habit This species, which often does not even resemble a cactus, grows like a shrub. Ordinary leaves emerge from the axils, in which the areoles are located. Only a few spines are present.

The flowers are produced singly or in groups, clusters, or panicles. They are white, yellowish, or pink.

Care *Pereskia* needs a moist, warm location during the summer. Light shade is preferable to full sun. In winter the plants should not be kept below 40°F (4.4°C) and should be moderately moist. For potting medium, this cactus needs humous, always moist cactus soil with a little loam and leaf mold.

Pereskia is very well-suited for being grown hydroponically.

Propagation Propagation is by cuttings.

Species *P. aculeata* climbs up to 33 feet (10 m) high. The stems are thin; the leaves are 2¾ inches (7 cm) long, short-stalked, and elongated. Few spines are found in the axils of the leaves. The flowers are 1¼ inches (4.5 cm) across and come in clusters. They are white, yellowish, or pink.

P. bleo grows 23 feet (7 m) high and branches heavily. The leaves are 8 inches (20 cm) long and 2 inches (5 cm) wide. They are produced on long stalks. The short, stout spines are black. The stalked flowers are rose-pink.

P. grandifolia is bushlike or treelike, and grows up to 16½ feet (5 m) high. The leaves are 5 inches (15 cm) long. The large flowers always appear at the end of the branch, and are rose-colored to pink. This species is very suitable as a rootstock for grafting.

P. sacharosa has purplish-pink flowers.

Pereskia, plant and flower

INFO

This genus was named in honor of N. C. F. de Peiresc (1580–1673), French councillor of state in Aix-en-Provence. For this reason, many well-known authors, not wishing to carry the mutilation of names into the current nomenclature, still use the earlier spelling *Peireskia*.

INFO

The flowers open at night; their odor of rotten onions or cabbage attracts bats for pollination.

Pilosocereus palmeri

Origin This "hairy cereus" is at home in Brazil. It was given this name as recently as 1956 by the two British botanists R. S. Byles and G. D. Rowley. Older nomenclatures have it listed under *Cephalocereus* and *Pilocereus*. Other species are also found in the literature under *Pseudopilocereus*.

Habit *Pilosocereus palmeri* grows up to 20 feet (6 m) high. The dark green stems remain slender. The ribs are rounded and have a glaucous bloom at the top. The spines, 1¼ inches (3 cm) long, are gray, being yellow only in older seedlings. The single central spine is 1¼ inches (3 cm) long and brownish. The crown has a heavy covering of hair extending down into the ribs. There is also a pseudocephalium, which is found at the tip of the stem. The fat flowers are pale pink.

Care This species is very vigorous. In summer it needs a sunny, airy location. The potting medium should contain gravel and loam and be slightly acidic. In winter it should be kept at 50°F (10°C).

Propagation Propagation is from seed.

Other Species *P. glaucescens* and *P. pentaëdrophorus* bear white flowers, while *P. werdermannianus* has greenish-white blossoms.

Pilosocereus palmeri

Rebutia
Dwarf Cactus

Origin This genus of tiny globular cacti, encompassing a great many species, is widespread in the northeast of Bolivia and in Argentina. They grow there at high elevations on usually barren soils. The German botanist K. M. Schumann (1851–1904) described the genus in 1895. He was a curator at the Botanical Museum in Berlin. Today this genus also includes species of *Aylostera, Digitorebutia, Lobivia, Mediolobivia, Sulcorebutia,* and *Weingartia.*

INFO
This genus was named in honor of the French vintner and cactus grower P. Rebut (1830–1898).

Rebutia albiflora

Rebutia deminuta

Rebutia famatinensis

Habit These are truly dwarfs among cacti, and the funnel-shaped flowers projecting at the sides of the tiny balls are a constant surprise. The spines are very fine and light, and the ribs resemble the tubercles of *Mammillaria*. *Rebutias* offshoot freely and thus form whole carpets of close-set blooming balls.

Care In summer these small cacti can be placed outdoors; they like an airy, sunny location. In winter they need a cool spot around 45°F (8°C) and very little water. In spring, start watering only when the first buds begin to show. Because they are sensitive to moisture, *rebutias* should be watered from the bottom. Regular cactus soil with an increased proportion of sand should be used as the potting medium. Fertilize fairly often in summer.

Rebutia heliosa

Propagation Propagation is from seed.

Species **R. albiflora** grows only an inch (2.5 cm) high. This species forms dense clumps through numerous off-shoots. The ribs have been converted into distant warts. The areoles are yellowish, the spines tiny. The central spines are brownish at the base. This species bears white flowers with delicate pink median stripes.

R. deminuta gets 2¼ inches (6 cm) high, forms numerous off-shoots, and has tubercles in rows. The bristles are white and have brown tips. The deep orange flowers are more than an inch (3 cm) in diameter.

R. famatinensis is a short cylinder and grows 1⅜ inches (3.5 cm) high. This species is freely offshooting. The whitish radial spines are bristle-like and soft; the brown central spines are just a little stouter and needlelike. This species bears blood-red flowers.

R. heliosa grows to only ¾ inch (2 cm). It has a large taproot and its ribs are twisted spirally and furnished with warts. It is striking that the white radial spines lie close to the plant body and point downward like a comb. No central spine is present. The orange flowers are 1½ inches (4 cm) in diameter.

R. kupperiana remains roundish and grows just 1¼ inches (3 cm) high. It forms only a few offshoots and is a dull green. The areoles are yellowish. The small radial spines are white with brown tips. The brown central spines are heavier and three times as long. R. kupperiana bears flowers that are a dark bronze-red.

R. marsoneri puts out its yellow flowers very early in spring. The spines on this 2-inch- (5-cm-) high cactus are variably colored, sometimes whitish but often also brownish.

Rebutia kupperiana

Rebutia marsoneri

Rebutia neocumingii

Rebutia rauschii

Rebutia steinbachii

R. neocumingii is a relatively large species, 4 inches (10 cm) in diameter. It does not form offshoots. The ribs are converted into rows of warts that are somewhat flat-edged. The whitish-yellow spines stand out. The 1-inch (2.5-cm) flowers are orange to golden yellow.

R. rauschii grows only ½ inch (1.5 cm) high but 1¼ inches (3 cm) wide. The body is a striking black-green to violet. The black radial spines are about ⅜ inch (1 cm) long and are curved downward like a claw. They lie close to the body of the plant. No central spines are present. The flowers are pink with white throats, and have red filaments.

R. steinbachii forms broad green cushions. This species grows 2¼ inches (6 cm) high. The black spines are 1 inch (2.5 cm) long; however, spines are often absent. The 1⅜-inch- (3.5-cm-) long flowers are scarlet red.

There are numerous other species. Here are a few of the best known:

R. glomeriseta bears yellow flowers.

R. krainziana has deep, dark red blossoms.

R. miniuscula and **R. senilis** also have red flowers.

R. arenacea bears golden-yellow flowers.

R. aureiflora has lemon-yellow or red to violet blooms.

R. einsteinii has yellow blossoms.

Rhipsalis
Wickerwork Cactus, Mistletoe
Cactus

Origin This genus not only does
not resemble a normal cactus, but
is so variable that it is difficult even
to classify the individual species of
the genus. And *Rhipsalis* is still another exception: It has been found
on Madagascar and in Sri Lanka as
sole representative of the Cactaceae. It is frequently found in the
forests of Brazil, South America,
and Florida. The genus was given
its name by the German physician
and botanist C. F. von Gärtner
(1772–1850). Current nomenclature also includes the genera *Ery-
throrhipsalis* and species of *Epiphyllum, Hatiora,* and *Lepismium*
in *Rhipsalis.*

Habit Whether thin as a thread
or thick as a finger, the stems have
one thing in common: They are
joined together in long joints,
branch in whorls, and grow exuberantly downward. Their joints
are often also flattened and resemble other leafy cacti. What is decorative about them is not their relatively small flowers but primarily
the fruits, which dress up the plant
like little round pearls in white,
red, or violet. *Rhipsalis* grows as an
epiphyte. It has no spines and only
a few bristles. Because of the conditions under which it grows in na-
ture, it has no succulent plant tissue, so it must always be watered
generously.

Care In summer *Rhipsalis* may be
placed outdoors in a shady spot; it
does not like direct sun. In winter it
should not be kept below about
50°F (10°C). It must be watered
regularly, therefore, and not be

Rhipsalis grandiflora

Flowers of
Rhipsalis grandiflora

Rhipsalis paradoxa

Rhipsalis pilocarpa

allowed to dry out. In winter, at the flowering season, the plant requires less water, so start cutting down on watering in the fall. As compared with other genera of cacti, this cactus is also an exception in terms of potting medium: It requires a soil rich in humus, to which some leaf mold may be added.

Propagation Propagation is from seed and by cuttings.

Species *R. clavata* grows erect at first and later becomes cascading. The stems are club-shaped, branching, and divided. The white flowers are bell-shaped.

R. crispata has wavy pendant stems. The cream-yellow flowers are produced laterally in clusters.

R. grandiflora is also known as the large-flowered *Rhipsalis.* It grows as a pendant bush, its slender stems getting no thicker than $^3/_8$ inch (1 cm). The flowers are an inch (2.5 cm) in diameter, are produced laterally, and are whitish with green stripes.

R. paradoxa grows like a bush. The short three-angled branches are joined at angles to one another. The individual segments are 2 inches (5 cm) long. The $^3/_4$-inch- (2-cm-) long white flowers emerge singly on the last part of the stem.

R. pilocarpa branches into whorls. The trailing stems grow $4^3/_4$ inches (12 cm) long and become bushy; they are only weakly ribbed, gray-green, and have bristles instead of spines. The scented pale yellow to greenish flowers are an inch (2.5 cm) wide.

Schlumbergera
Christmas cactus

Origin The French cactus authority A. C. Lemaire (1800–1871) established *Schlumbergera,* the old-
est genus of the easily confused
leafy cacti, in 1858. It comes from
Brazil and is found there as an
epiphyte at altitudes of 1,300 to
6,550 feet (400 to 2,000 m) above
sea level. Several species formerly
were listed under *Epiphyllanthus*
or *Zygocactus.*

Habit The Christmas cactus
grows like a bush with stems
1–2 inches (3–5 cm) long; these
are flattened, notched leaflike on
both edges, and joined end to
end. The flowers are very large;
they appear in various shades of
red and pink and open during
the day.

Care *Schlumbergera* needs more
shade than sun; at the same time,
it should be kept warm and moist.
It requires a potting medium of
slightly acidic soil rich in nutrients. After blooming, the plant
needs a dormant period of about
4 weeks, during which time it
must stay very dry. A bright room
at a temperature of 50°F (10°C) is
satisfactory as the normal winter
location.

Propagation Propagation is from
seed and by cuttings.

Species *S. russeliana* grows up
to 3 feet (1 m) high. The trunk is
round-jointed, the 1³⁄₈-inch- (3.5-
cm-) long stems are light green,
and their central nerve is clearly
visible. A few hairlike spines are
found at the end of the joints. The
bright, dark red flowers measure
2¹⁄₄ inches (5.5 cm).

TIP

The blooming
period can be
extended if
the plants are
put in a cooler
place once the
buds have set.

Schlumbergera
hybrid

Schlumbergera
truncata

S. truncata is the wild form of the Christmas cactus. It grows as a small shrub about a foot (30 cm) high. The plant has multiply jointed stems that grow 1¾ inches (4.5 cm) long and are toothed at the sides. The areoles are rather feltlike, the bristles short and fine. The 3-inch (8-cm) flowers appear at the ends of the stems in twos or sometimes even in threes, in pink, red, or violet-red.

S. orssichiana has 3½-inch (9-cm) crimson-red to magenta flowers.

Various **S. hybrids,** available on the market in numerous flower colors, are the actual Christmas cacti. Their flowers, which are often gorgeous, have pink, red, violet, or two-toned shades (see also photograph on page 154).

Schlumbergera hybrids

INFO

The discoverer of *S. orssichiana,* Beatrix Orssich of Teresópolis (Brazil), created lovely species hybrids, called *S. x seginae.* Their parents are *S. orssichiana* and various varieties of the Christmas cactus. This is how bicolor (red/white) flowers have been obtained.

Sclerocactus

Origin This genus is at home in the southwestern United States. According to the current nomenclature, it includes representatives of *Ancistrocactus, Coloradoa, Echinocactus, Echinomastus, Glandulicactus, Hamatocactus, Mammillaria, Neolloydia, Pediocactus, Toumeya,* and *Theocactus.* The genus *Sclerocactus* was named and described by the two well-known cactus authorities N. Lord Britton (1859–1934) and J. N. Rose (1862–1928).

Habit This cactus is globular to cylindrical, and occasionally also egg-shaped. Its spines are long, usually flattened, sometimes hooked. The flowers have a bell-funnel shape and open in the daytime.

Care Since *Sclerocactus* comes from hot, dry areas, it should be kept in a warm, sunny location during the summer. A very sandy cactus soil is advisable as the potting medium, because *Sclerocactus* does not like "wet feet." In winter the cactus is best kept very cool (around 32°F [0°C]) and dry. Grafted plants definitely are more vigorous.

Propagation Propagation is from seed and by grafting.

Species *S. intertextus* grows close to 5 inches (12 cm) high and then has a diameter of more than 2 inches (6 cm). It is a lively green. Its woolly crown is slightly depressed.

Sclerocactus intertextus

Sclerocactus papyracanthus

Sclerocactus unguispinus

The numerous radial spines are intertwined and lie close to the body. The central spines, on the other hand, stand straight up and have a reddish hue. The very pale purple to whitish flowers have a white margin and measure an inch (2.5 cm) in diameter.

S. papyracanthus is not called Grama Grass Cactus without reason: Its whorled and projecting spines are a light brown, so that it resembles the grass found in the plains. The flowers grow ⅜ inch (1 cm) across and have a silky white sheen.

S. unguispinus is globular and grows to about 4 inches (10 cm). The spined crown is woolly. Its ribs are warty. Some of the white radial spines are intertwined. The horn-colored central spines are heavier. One of them grows about 1½ inches (4 cm) long and projects downward; it is dark brown and curved like a claw. The flowers, which are ¾ inch (2 cm), are greenish with a red-tinged center.

S. erectocentrus is cylindrical and bluish gray. Its flowers are pink.

S. johnsonii has reddish spines and 2½-inch (6.5-cm) flesh-pink blossoms, which may also shade into white and purplish pink.

S. mariposensis bears flowers in shades of pinkish brown.

Selenicereus
Climbing Cactus

Origin Almost 30 species of this genus are found in Central and South America. The legendary Queen of the Night is one of these. The genus was given its name by the two North American botanists N. Lord Britton (1859–1934) and J. N. Rose (1862–1928). Older sources list several species under the genera *Cereus, Cryptocereus, Deamia,* and *Strophocactus.*

Habit *Selenicereus* grows shrub-like and develops long thin stems with numerous aerial roots. The stems are angular and usually spined. The spines are short, often absent on new growth. The most striking thing about this genus is the very large flowers, some of which can reach a length of more than one foot (30 cm). In some species, they have a strong smell of vanilla. Each flower opens its petals for only one night. In the evening it unfolds to form a large garland of rays; when morning comes, the show is already over.

Propagation Propagation is from seed and by cuttings.

Care Indoors *Selenicereus* should be kept in bright light, but not in strong sun. Its long stems may be allowed to climb up a trellis or given some other support. The plant grows so exuberantly that it can spread over a window after only a few years. *Selenicereus* should be watered sparingly in summer, too, with water that has been allowed to stand. Keep this cactus dry and cool (around 40°F [4.4°C]) in winter. Use cactus soil with a little

INFO

In 1991 Dr. W. Hoffmann of Greisenheim, Germany, discovered the species *S. megalanthus,* which plays a great role as a cultivated plant in Bolivia and Colombia. The fruits, called *pitaya,* are very tasty.

Selenicereus grandiflorus

Selenicereus hamatus

TIP

Selenicereus forms aerial roots, so that sometimes no trellis or framework is required on rough walls.

humus as the potting medium.

Species *S. grandiflorus* is the Queen of the Night, so-called for its immense, strongly scented flowers, up to a foot (30 cm) across, which are produced on the plant in large numbers and are really spectacular. The outer petals are brown, the inner ones white to cream-colored. The stems are only an inch (2.5 cm) thick and are truly climbing. Their few yellowish spines are quite irregular and soon fall off.

S. pteranthus is called the Princess of the Night because it has winged, pure white flowers that are just as lovely and may reach 13 inches (33 cm) in diameter. However, they are not scented.

S. hamatus, with blossoms almost 16 inches (40 cm) long and a foot (30 cm) wide, unquestionably has the largest flowers in this genus. They are brown to greenish on the outside and white on the inside.

S. macdonaldiae forms very long, thin stems of up to 3 feet (1 m). The more than 13-inch (35-cm) flowers have reddish or orange recurved sepals and pure white petals.

S. coniflorus has spines almost ½ inch (1 cm) long that stick out like rays on the thin stems. The white flowers are a delicate green at the base.

S. inermis is completely spineless, a few bristles being present only at first. The white flowers are reddish at the base and grow up to 6 inches (15 cm) in diameter.

S. kunthianus has light green stems and stiff, crisscrossing spines. The scented white flowers grow up to 9 inches (23 cm) in diameter and are pink on the outside.

S. nelsonii and *S. pringlei* have 8-inch (20-cm) white flowers.

Selenicereus macdonaldiae

Stenocereus

Origin This columnar cactus is indigenous to the southern United States and to Mexico. The Italian gardener and cactus researcher V. Riccobono (1861–1943) is responsible for its name. Some species are still found under *Cereus, Hertrichocereus, Isolatocereus, Lemaireocereus, Machaerocereus, Marshallocereus, Pachycereus,* and *Ritterocereus* in older sources.

Habit This columnar *Cereus* usually branches from the bottom but seldom forms a crown. It may be erect and grow up to 50 feet (15 m) high, but there are also low-growing species. The stems are usually dark green. The bell-shaped flowers open at night, emerging around the top from a ring of bristles.

Care In summer *Stenocereus* requires a sunny, warm, and open space where it is not cramped. Since it does not like "wet feet," the potting soil, without much humus, should be mixed with a little sand. And be careful about watering: better too little than too much. In winter the cactus should generally be kept cool (around 32°F [0°C]) and dry.

Propagation Propagation is from seed and by cuttings.

Species *S. dumortieri* grows 50 feet (15 m) high, with the trunk only about 3 feet (1 m) high, and has a diameter of one foot (30 cm). The stems are bluish green. The spines have a yellowish-white coloration, the central spines growing about 1¼ inches (3 cm) long. The 2-inch (5-cm) white flowers are brown-red on the outside.

TIP

To keep water from standing at the root collar, I place a layer of sand on the surface of the soil.

Stenocereus dumortieri

Stenocereus eruca

Stenocereus pruinosus

Stenocereus thurberi

S. eruca grows creeping and may reach 10 feet (3 m) in length. Its stems, around 3 inches (8 cm) thick, root laterally, the tips rising up again. It is not greatly branched. The thick white to gray spines are flattened. The white flowers grow about 6 inches (15 cm) long.

S. pruinosus may grow 23 feet (7 m) high; it has a powdery glaucous and white bloom at the tips of the stems. The ribs are sharply furrowed lengthwise. The spines are gray-brown with a reddish tip. The central spine is 1¼ inches (3 cm) long and distinctly heavier. The flowers, almost 4 inches (10 cm) in diameter, are white with pink shading.

S. thurberi is known as the Organ-pipe Cactus, because its numerous stems are not clearly differentiated at the base, but stand close together and grow upward in wide curves. This cactus grows 23 feet (7 m) high and usually remains trunkless. The 3-inch (7.5-cm) flower is light purple.

S. beneckei bears ivory flowers with a reddish sheen.

S. queretaroensis grows tree-like and has 3½-inch (9-cm) light red blossoms.

S. stellatus has pale pink cylindrical flowers.

Stephanocereus leucostele

Origin This white-columned *Cereus,* which was named by the Thuringian succulent researcher A. Berger (1871–1931), comes from dry forests in northern Brazil. Other, older sources list this species under *Cephalocereus* or *Pilocereus.*

Habit This slender columnar cactus grows 10 feet (3 m) high and attains a diameter of at most 3 inches (8 cm). It looks very light and white, because the areoles are covered with white hairs and its spines are white. The long central spines, however, sometimes get slightly yellowish. A white woolly cephalium and long, dense, golden-yellow bristles develop on mature plants. The latter remain as a crown of bristles, while the cephalium is formed anew each year. The white, bell-like flowers grow to $2^3/_4$ inches (7 cm) and are yellowish at the bottom.

Care It is important for *Stephanocereus leucostele* to have a sunny to semisunny location with plenty of fresh air all summer long. The potting medium used is cactus soil to which a little loam has been added. In winter the plant should stay cool, 32°F (0°C) being satisfactory. At the same time, it should be kept almost dry.

Propagation Propagation is from seed and by grafting.

Other Species The only other known species of the genus is **S. leutzelburgii,** with unbranched trunks.

Stephanocereus leucostele

Stetsonia coryne

Origin This genus comes from the northwest of Argentina and the south of Bolivia. It was described by the two botanists N. Lord Britton (1859–1934) and J. N. Rose (1862–1928). This species was formerly listed under the genus *Cereus.*

Stetsonia coryne

TIP

Stetsonia comes from very dry pampas and grows on mounds, so water it very moderately.

Habit This bluish-green columnar cactus grows like a tree, forming a broad crown. *Stetsonia coryne* may grow 26 feet (8 m) high; its trunk then has a diameter of something like 16 inches (40 cm), the stems growing 2 feet (60 cm) long. The brownish-yellow or white, sometimes black-tipped, spines grow 1¼ inches (3 cm) long. The strong thick central spine grows 2 inches (5 cm) long and projects from the other spines. The white, 6-inch (15-cm) flowers open at night.

Care *Stetsonia* likes to be kept in a very sunny and warm spot in summer. Since it is somewhat sensitive to moisture, it requires a porous, sandy soil. In winter keep it dry and at a temperature of about 32°F (0°C).

Propagation Propagation is from seed and by cuttings.

Other Species Only this one species is known.

Strombocactus disciformis

Origin This cactus comes from the dry regions of eastern Mexico. It grows there in barren scree, and has even been found growing in crevices. The botanists N. L. Britton (1859–1934) and J. N. Rose (1862–1928) gave this genus its name in 1922. Older sources listed this cactus under the genera *Echinocactus, Mammillaria,* and

Strombocactus disciformis

Ariocarpus. Other species, formerly classified under *Strombocactus,* are today considered to belong to *Neolloydia.*

Habit This flattened-globular, gray-green cactus usually grows no bigger than 3 inches (8 cm). The ribs are converted into thick warts. *Strombocactus* has only a few bristlelike spines. These soon fall off, only a few remaining near the crown, from which the 1 1/2-inch (4-cm) white flowers also emerge.

Care This cactus needs full sun and lots of heat. It does not like "wet feet"; the potting medium, which should contain no additional humus, must include plenty of sand and gravel.

Propagation Propagation is from seed. Very young cuttings are often grafted on *Pereskiopsis,* because they then bloom in the second year.

Other Species The genus consists of only this one species.

Thelocactus

Origin *Thelocactus* is found in Texas, New Mexico, and northern Mexico. The two botanists N. L. Britton (1859–1934) and J. N. Rose (1862–1928) gave the genus the name generally accepted today. In older sources species were listed under the genera *Echinocactus, Ferocactus, Gymnocactus,* and *Hamatocactus.* Several earlier *Thelocactus* species are today considered to belong to *Neolloydia.*

Thelocactus heterochromus

Thelocactus rinconensis

TIP

Water *Strombocactus* sparingly in summer too!

INFO

In most species of *Thelocactus* the fruits burst open when the seeds are ripe, so that the seeds are scattered and thus provide for widespread distribution of the species.

Habit This cactus generally is globular to elongated. Its ribs are warty. The spines are strong and sometimes coarsely fibrous. They range from white and yellow through red all the way to brown—and this on one and the same plant! The central spines are often flattened.

Care This vigorous cactus prefers a sunny, warm location. It does not tolerate "wet feet"; the loamy potting medium should contain a large proportion of sand or gravel. In winter *Thelocactus* should be kept at a temperature of 32°F (0°C) and almost dry. But the fibrous roots should never be allowed to dry out completely!

Propagation Propagation is from seed and by grafting of cuttings.

Species *T. heterochromus* is a squat globular cactus that grows 6 inches (15 cm) high and is blue-green. The ribs are roundish warts. They shrivel up noticeably in winter. The white areoles form a contrast to the reddish to brownish spines. Its violet flowers reach 4 inches (10 cm) in diameter.

T. rinconensis is gray to blue-green, becomes 4.5 inches (12 cm) thick, and has ribs that are very warty. The radial spines are ½ inch (1.5 cm) long and central spines are absent. The white flowers reach 1½ inches (4 cm) in diameter. (Formerly *T. lophothele*).

Thelocactus setispinus

T. setispinus is a well-known species that at first is globular and later becomes elongated. It reaches a size of about 6 inches (15 cm). The variably long radial spines are brown and white. With their lighter hooked tips, the longer dark brown central spines are striking. The flowers get 2¾ inches (7 cm) long and are a silken glossy yellow with a red center.

T. tulensis reaches a size of 4¾ inches (12 cm), is globular, and does not elongate much when mature. Its dark green body has pronounced conical warts. It has brown, later white, radial spines and 1½-inch (4-cm) straight or curved central spines, which are horn-colored and have dark tips. The silvery white to pink flowers reach a size of 1½ inches (4 cm); their median stripes are crimson.

T. bicolor has bright purplish-pink flowers.

T. conothelos bears red-violet blossoms.

T. hexaëdrophorus has white flowers.

T. leucacanthus bears yellow blossoms.

Uebelmannia pectinifera

Origin This cactus is at home in the Brazilian state of Minas Gerais, in the Serrado Espinhaço. It grows there at elevations of 3,300 feet (1,000 m), in almost pure white quartz sand. Sometimes young plants are completely covered with quartz sand. The Dutch cactus specialist, A. F. H. Buining (1901–1980), described this genus. It was only discovered in 1966 and has not yet received much scientific study.

Thelocactus tulensis

Flowers of *Uebelmannia pectinifera*

Habit The globular, slightly cylindrical cactus has ribs running vertically. *Uebelmannia pectinifera* can grow 20 inches (50 cm) high and about 6 inches (15 cm) thick. The body of the plant is red-brown and is covered by a waxy, gray coating. The dark brown spines stand erect in close-set clusters. The flowers remain small and are greenish yellow.

Care *Uebelmannia* can stay in a sunny location in summer but needs high humidity. The potting medium should contain plenty of gravel; no additional humus is required. In winter the plants are best kept dry and at a temperature above 40°F (4.4°C).

Propagation Propagation is from seed.

Other Species In some cases, the forms identified in older sources as individual species, such as the variety *pseudopectinifera,* shown in the photograph at left, exhibit only very slight differences and, therefore, are now all classified as *U. pectinifera.*

U. buiningii is usually red-brown and strongly ribbed. The 4 to 8 spines are brownish and curved and have dark tips. The flowers are yellow.

Uebelmannia pectinifera

Short Cactus Glossary

Aerial roots: Roots that grow from stems above soil level (e.g., in *epiphytes*).

Areole: Telescoped center of growth in cacti. Areoles are also described as cushion-like structures from which spines, bristles, and hairs generally grow. Flowers and side stems also arise here. Exception: *Mammillaria.*

Axils: Growing points lying at the base of tubercles (e.g., in *Mammillaria*), from which arise hairs, bristles, side shoots, and flowers.

Callus: Protective tissue forming over a wound.

Central spine: Differs clearly from other spines, is usually longer and stouter, often also of a different color.

Cephalium: Flower-bearing region, which has densely packed hair, many bristles, or woolly growth.

Chlorophyll: Green plant pigment, found in the chloroplasts.

Cristate form: Abnormal growth, shaped like a cockscomb, in which the growing point has become a crest.

Epiphytes: Plants that grow on trees, but without drawing nourishment from them like parasites. They cling to the tree by hold-fasts, some also having long hanging nutrient roots (aerial roots).

Genus: Taxonomic term denoting several closely related species.

Glochids: Fine bristly spines, usually barbed, which are easily detached (e.g., in *Opuntia, Pereskia*).

Spines of a *Coryphantha.*

Cephalium in *Melocactus.*

Cristate form in *Mammillaria.*

Left: The vascular bundles, arranged in a ring, are clearly visible.

Right: Pectinate spines in *Pelecyphora*.

Central spine in *Ferocactus*.

Schlumbergera hybrid, bicolor selection

Hybrid: Result of a cross between two different species (e.g., in *Epiphyllum*).

Monstrous form: Irregular growth form, in which ribs and areoles are modified, (e.g., in *Cereus peruvianus* 'Monstrosus').

Ovaries: Lowermost parts of a cactus flower, which act as seed chambers.

Pectinate spines: Spines spreading horizontally on either side on elongated areoles.

Petals: Inner circle of flower leaves (corolla).

Radial spines: These are clustered around the central spine and differ distinctly from the latter in color and shape.

Ribs: Ridges, usually vertical, on the body of a cactus.

Sepals: Outer circle of flower leaves (calyx).

Shallow-rooted plants: Plants having a root system lying close to the surface of the soil.

Species: Basic taxonomic unit (unit of classification).

Spines: In cacti, modified leaves, roots, or shoots that are firmly joined with the body of the plant.

Stomata: Openings in the outer skin serving for gas exchange and transpiration.

Succulent: Fleshy, storing water.

Thorns: Found not in cacti but, for example, in roses. They are protuberances of the outer skin and, unlike spines, are easily detachable.

Vascular bundle: Strands of tissue made up of longitudinal cells, in which water, nutrients and substances formed by the plant are transported.

Cactus Societies

UNITED STATES

Cactus and Succulent Society of America, Inc.
P. O. Box 2615
Pahrump, NV 89041-2615

The Society has affiliates throughout the United States as well as internationally. Its web site may be accessed through http://www.cactus-mall.com for detailed information.

Cactus and Succulent Research (ACSR)
8 S. Cactus Lane
Bisbee, Arizona 85603

CANADA

Burnaby Cactus and Succulent Club
4261 Gatenby Avenue
Burnaby, British Columbia V5G 3M8

Toronto Cactus and Succulent Club
9091 Eighth Line Road, RR2
Georgetown, Ontario L7G 4S5

Desert Plant Society of Vancouver
1550 William Street
Vancouver, British Columbia V5L 2R2

Victoria Cactus and Succulent Society
3903 Cedar Hills Cross Road
Victoria, British Columbia V8P 2N3

Sources of Supply

UNITED STATES

Abbey Gardens
4620 Carpenteria Avenue
Carpenteria, CA 90313
(805) 684-5112

Bach's Cactus Farm, Inc.
11550 East Speedway
Tucson, AZ 85748
(602) 749-2285

Mesa Garden
P.O. Box 72
Belen, NM 87002

CANADA

Vandusen Gardens
5251 Oak Street
Vancouver, British Columbia
V6M 4H1
(604) 525-5315

Additional information may be found through the Internet, under keyword "cactus and succulents".

Literature

I can recommend the following for further reading:

Benson, Lyman D.: *Cacti of the United States and Canada.* Stanford University Press, Stanford, California, 1982.

Britton, Nathaniel L. & Rose, J. N.: *Cactaceae: Descriptions and Illustrations of Plants of the Cactus Family, 4 Vols.* Dover Press, Mineola, New York, 1937.

Griffiths, Mark: *The New Royal Horticultural Society Dictionary, Index of Garden Plants.* Macmillan Press, London, 1994.

Hewitt, Terry: *The Complete Book of Cacti and Succulents.* DK Publishing, Inc., New York, 1997.

Innes, Clive: *Cacti, A Wisley Handbook.* Cassell Educational Limited, London, 1988, for the Royal Horticultural Society.

Innes, Clive & Glass, Charles: *The Illustrated Encyclopedia of Cacti.* Knickerbocker Press, Edison, New Jersey, 1997.

Lamb, Edgar & Brian: *Colorful Cacti of the American Deserts.* Macmillan Publishing Co., Inc., New York, 1974.

Preston-Mafham, Rod & Ken: *Cacti: The Illustrated Dictionary.* Timber Press, Inc., Portland, Oregon, 1997.

Riha, Jan & Subik, Rudolf: *Illustrated Encyclopedia of Cacti and Other Succulents,* ed. Kenneth A. Beckett, Chartwell Books, New Jersey, 1993.

Rowley, Gordon Douglas: *History of Succulent Plants.* Strawberry Press, Mill Valley, California, 1997.

Photographs

Becherer: p. 1, 2/3, 4, 10, 12, 13 top right, 13 center left, 13 bottom left, 13 bottom right, 14 top, 14 bottom left, 15 bottom right, 14/15 bottom, 15 top left, 17, 18, 20, 21, 22, 23 top, 23 bottom, 24, 25, 26 left, 26 top right, 26 bottom right, 28 top left, 28 top right, 28 bottom, 31 top, 31 bottom, 32 top left, 32 top right, 32 bottom, 33 top, 33 center, 33 bottom, 34 top, 35, 37, 39, 40 top, 41 top, 41 bottom, 43 bottom, 49 top, 50, 51, 52 bottom, 56 bottom, 59 top, 59 bottom, 60 bottom, 61 top, 68 top, 69 top, 69 bottom, 73 bottom, 74, 75 top, 75 bottom, 78, 79 top, 79 bottom, 80 top, 82 bottom, 83 bottom, 85 bottom, 89 top, 89 bottom, 98 bottom, 101 top, 101 bottom, 102, 110 top, 117 bottom, 119 bottom, 122 bottom, 123 top, 129 top, 129 bottom, 131 (large photograph), 137 (large photograph), 137 (filler), 139 top, 140 top, 140 center, 140 bottom, 144, 151 bottom, 153 top, 153 bottom, 153 center, 154 top left, 154 center, 154 bottom

Bušek: p. 6, 8, 9 top, 9 bottom left, 9 bottom right, 11 bottom, 13 top left, 16, 19, 34 bottom, 62 top, 62 bottom, 63 top, 63 bottom, 71 bottom, 76 bottom, 109 bottom, 117 top, 118 bottom, 131 (filler), 152, 154 top right

Haage: p. 38, 57 top, 57 bottom, 90 bottom, 130 bottom, 143 bottom, 147 top

Schmied: p. 30

Strauss: p. 27, 36 top, 36 bottom

Graphics: Daniela Farnhammer
Cover design: Studio Schübel, Munich
Cover photographs: Hermann Eisenbeiss
Frontispiece: *Mammillaria guelzowiana*
Back cover: *chinocereus pectinatus* (left), *Blossfeldia liliputana* (center), *Echinocereus mamillosa* var. *kermesina* (right)

English translation © Copyright 2000 by Barron's Educational Series, Inc.

Title of the original German edition:
DAS BLV KAKTEEN-BUCH
© 1998 BLV Verlagsgesellschaft mbH, München/GERMANY

Translated from the German by Helen Hasselriis.

All rights reserved.
No part of this book may be reproduced in any form, by photostat, microfilm, xerography, or any other means, or incorporated into any information retrieval system, electronic or mechanical, without the written permission of the copyright owner.

All inquiries should be addressed to:
Barron's Educational Series, Inc.
250 Wireless Boulevard
Hauppauge, New York 11788
http://www.barronseduc.com

Library of Congress Catalog Card No.
99-47359

ISBN-13: 978-0-7641-1226-3
ISBN-10: 0-7641-1226-0

Library of Congress Cataloging-in-Publication Data

Manke, Elisabeth.
  [BLV Kakteen-buch. English]
  Cactus : the most beautiful species and their care / Elisabeth Manke.
      p. cm.
  Includes bibliographical references (p.).
  ISBN 0-7641-1226-0
  1. Cactus.   I. Title.

SB438 .M2713 2000   99-47359
635.9'3356—dc21   CIP

PRINTED IN CHINA
9